Communications in Computer and Information Science   964

Commenced Publication in 2007
Founding and Former Series Editors:
Phoebe Chen, Alfredo Cuzzocrea, Xiaoyong Du, Orhun Kara, Ting Liu,
Krishna M. Sivalingam, Dominik Ślęzak, Takashi Washio, and Xiaokang Yang

More information about this series at http://www.springer.com/series/7899

Amit Majumdar · Ritu Arora (Eds.)

Software Challenges to Exascale Computing

Second Workshop, SCEC 2018
Delhi, India, December 13–14, 2018
Proceedings

 Springer

Editors
Amit Majumdar
San Diego Supercomputer Center
University of California, San Diego
La Jolla, CA, USA

Ritu Arora
Texas Advanced Computing Center
The University of Texas at Austin
Austin, TX, USA

ISSN 1865-0929   ISSN 1865-0937 (electronic)
Communications in Computer and Information Science
ISBN 978-981-13-7728-0   ISBN 978-981-13-7729-7 (eBook)
https://doi.org/10.1007/978-981-13-7729-7

This Springer imprint is published by the registered company Springer Nature Singapore Pte Ltd.
The registered company address is: 152 Beach Road, #21-01/04 Gateway East, Singapore 189721, Singapore

Preface

Supercomputers are used to power discoveries and to reduce the time-to-results in a wide variety of disciplines such as engineering, physical sciences, and healthcare. They are globally considered as vital for staying competitive in defense, the financial sector, several mainstream businesses, and even agriculture. An integral requirement for enabling the usage of the supercomputers, like any other computer, is the availability of the software. Scalable and efficient software is typically required for optimally using the large-scale supercomputing platforms, and thereby, effectively leveraging the investments in the advanced CyberInfrastructure (CI). However, developing and maintaining such software is challenging due to several factors, such as, (1) no well-defined processes or guidelines for writing software that can ensure high-performance on supercomputers, and (2) shortfall of trained workforce having skills in both software engineering and supercomputing. With the rapid advancement in the computer architecture discipline, the complexity of the processors that are used in the supercomputers is also increasing, and, in turn, the task of developing efficient software for supercomputers is further becoming challenging and complex.

To mitigate the aforementioned challenges, there is a need for a common platform that brings together different stakeholders from the areas of supercomputing and software engineering. To provide such a platform, the second workshop on Software Challenges to Exascale Computing (SCEC) was organized in Delhi, India, during December 13–14, 2018.

The SCEC 2018 workshop informed participants about the challenges in large-scale HPC software development and steered them in the direction of building international collaborations for finding solutions to those challenges. The workshop provided a forum through which hardware vendors and software developers can communicate with each other and influence the architecture of the next-generation supercomputing systems and the supporting software stack. By fostering cross-disciplinary associations, the workshop served as a stepping-stone towards innovations in the future.

We are very grateful to the Organizing and Program Committees (listed below), the sponsors (US National Science Foundation, Indian National Supercomputing Mission, Atos, Mellanox, Centre for Development of Advanced Computing, San Diego Supercomputing Center, Texas Advanced Computing Center), and the participants for their contributions to making the SCEC 2018 workshop a success.

March 2019

Amit Majumdar
Ritu Arora

Organization

Organizing Committee

Amitava Majumdar (General Chair)	San Diego Supercomputing Center (SDSC), UC San Diego, USA
Ritu Arora (General Chair)	Texas Advanced Computing Center (TACC), UT Austin, USA
Sharda Dixit (Program Co-chair)	Center of Development of Advanced Computing (C-DAC), Pune, India
Anil Kumar Gupta (Program Co-chair)	Center of Development of Advanced Computing (C-DAC), Pune, India
Vinai Kumar Singh (Event Promotion)	Indraprastha Engineering College, Ghaziabad, India
Venkatesh Shenoi (Communications Chair)	Center of Development of Advanced Computing (C-DAC), Pune, India
Vinodh Kumar Markapuram	Center of Development of Advanced Computing (C-DAC), Pune, India
Abhishek Das	Center of Development of Advanced Computing (C-DAC), Pune, India
Gaurav Rajput	Neilson Global Holdings, India
Sweta Anmulwar	Center of Development of Advanced Computing (C-DAC), Pune, India
Richa Jha	Center of Development of Advanced Computing (C-DAC), Pune, India

Technical Program Committee

Amit Ruhela	Ohio State University, USA
Amitava Majumdar	San Diego Supercomputing Center (SDSC), UC San Diego, USA
Anil Kumar Gupta	Center of Development of Advanced Computing (C-DAC), Pune, India
Antonio Gomez	Intel, Hillsboro, USA
Amarjeet Sharma	Center of Development of Advanced Computing (C-DAC), Pune, India
Devangi Parekh	University of Texas at Austin, USA
Krishna Muriki	Lawrence Berkeley National Laboratory, USA
Lars Koesterke	Texas Advanced Computing Center (TACC), UT Austin, USA
Manu Awasthi	IIT-Gandhinagar, India
Mahidhar Tatineni	San Diego Supercomputer Center (SDSC), UC San Diego, USA

Nisha Agarwal	Center of Development of Advanced Computing (C-DAC), Pune, India
Purushotham Bangalore	University of Alabama at Birmingham, USA
Ritu Arora	Texas Advanced Computing Center (TACC), UT Austin, USA
Robert Sinkovits	San Diego Supercomputing Center (SDSC), UC San Diego, USA
Si Liu	Texas Advanced Computing Center (TACC), UT Austin, USA
Soham Ghosh	Intel, India
Subhashini Sivagnanam	San Diego Supercomputer Center (SDSC), UC San Diego, USA
Sukrit Sondhi	Fulcrum Worldwide, USA
Tajendra Singh	University of California, Los Angeles (UCLA), USA
Venkatesh Shenoi	Center of Development of Advanced Computing (C-DAC), Pune, India
Vinai Kumar Singh	Indraprastha Engineering College, Ghaziabad, India

Webmaster

Gerald Joshua	Texas Advanced Computing Center (TACC), USA

Contents

High-Productivity Tools and Frameworks

Scientific Applications

Corrfunc: Blazing Fast Correlation Functions with AVX512F SIMD Intrinsics

Manodeep Sinha[1,3]([⊠])(iD) and Lehman Garrison[2](iD)

[1] SA 101, Centre for Astrophysics and Supercomputing,
Swinburne University of Technology, 1 Alfred Street, Hawthorn, VIC 3122, Australia
msinha@swin.edu.au
[2] Harvard-Smithsonian Center for Astrophysics,
60 Garden Street, MS-10, Cambridge, MA 02138, USA
[3] ARC Centre of Excellence for All Sky Astrophysics in 3 Dimensions (ASTRO 3D),
Research School for Astronomy & Astrophysics, Australian National University,
Mt Stromlo Observatory, Cotter Road, Weston Creek, ACT 2611, Australia

Abstract. Correlation functions are widely used in extra-galactic astrophysics to extract insights into how galaxies occupy dark matter halos and in cosmology to place stringent constraints on cosmological parameters. A correlation function fundamentally requires computing pair-wise separations between two sets of points and then computing a histogram of the separations. Corrfunc is an existing open-source, high-performance software package for efficiently computing a multitude of correlation functions. In this paper, we will discuss the SIMD AVX512F kernels within Corrfunc, capable of processing 16 floats or 8 doubles at a time. The latest manually implemented Corrfunc AVX512F kernels show a speedup of up to ~4× relative to compiler-generated code for double-precision calculations. The AVX512F kernels show ~1.6× speedup relative to the AVX kernels and compares favorably to a theoretical maximum of 2×. In addition, by pruning pairs with too large of a minimum possible separation, we achieve a ~5–10% speedup across all the SIMD kernels. Such speedups highlight the importance of programming explicitly with SIMD vector intrinsics for complex calculations that can not be efficiently vectorized by compilers. Corrfunc is publicly available at https://github.com/manodeep/Corrfunc/.

Keywords: Correlation functions · AVX512 · SIMD intrinsics ·
Molecular dynamics · Spatial distance histograms · Applications

1 Introduction

Dark matter halos are spatially distributed in the Universe based on the values of the cosmological parameters in the ΛCDM cosmological model. Galaxies live in dark matter halos, but how these galaxies populate halos depends on a complex interplay between various astrophysical processes. We constrain this 'galaxy-halo connection' by statistically comparing the spatial distribution of observed and

© Springer Nature Singapore Pte Ltd. 2019
A. Majumdar and R. Arora (Eds.): SCEC 2018, CCIS 964, pp. 3–20, 2019.
https://doi.org/10.1007/978-981-13-7729-7_1

modeled galaxies. One such commonly used statistical measure is the correlation function.

A correlation function is the measure of the excess probability of finding a pair of galaxies at a certain separation, compared to that of an Poisson process. The simplest correlation function is a 3-D spatial one—$\xi(r)$:

$$dP = n_g(r)\left[1 + \xi(r)\right]dV, \tag{1}$$

where dP is the excess probability of finding a pair of galaxies, $n_g(r)$ is the number density of galaxies, and $\xi(r)$ is the correlation function. In practice, to calculate the correlation function, we need to count the number of galaxy-pairs found at a different separations. The separations themselves are typically discretized as a histogram; as such, calculating a correlation function amounts to calculating pairwise separations followed by a spatial distance histogram. We then need to compare these pair counts with the number expected from randomly distributed points for the same histogram bins. $\xi(r)$ is frequently calculated with the following [5]:

$$\xi(r) = \frac{N_{DD}(r)}{N_{RR}(r)} - 1, \tag{2}$$

where $N_{DD}(r)$ and $N_{RR}(r)$ are respectively the number of "data-data" and "random-random" pairs in the histogram bin of separation $r + \delta r$.

In additional to the full 3-D separation r, the spatial separations can be split into two components—typically a line-of-sight (π) and a projected separation (r_p). The line-of-sight direction is arbitrary but is usually chosen to be a coordinate axis. When the separations are split into two components, the correlation function is computed as a 2D histogram of pair-counts, referred to as $\xi(r_p, \pi)$. The two-point projected correlation function, $w_p(r_p)$, is simply the integral of $\xi(r_p, \pi)$ along the line-of-sight and defined as:

$$w_p(r_p) = 2\int_0^{\pi_{\max}} \xi(r_p, \pi)d\pi \tag{3}$$

For the remainder of the paper we will focus on these two correlation functions—$w_p(r_p)$ and $\xi(r)$.

A correlation function can be used to statistically compare any theoretically generated set of mock galaxies to the observed galaxy clustering. Such a comparison is frequently done within a Monte Carlo Markov Chain process [7]. For any reasonable MCMC estimates of the posterior, we would need a large number of evaluations of the correlation function. Hence a faster correlation function code is a key component for cutting edge astrophysical research.

In [8] we showed that Corrfunc is *at least* 2× faster than all existing bespoke correlation function codes. Corrfunc achieves such high-performance by refining the entire domain into cells, and then handling cell pairs with bespoke SIMD kernels targeting various instruction set architectures. In [8], we presented three different kernels targeting three different instruction sets – AVX, SSE and the Fallback kernels. In this work, we will present AVX512F kernels and additional optimizations.

1.1   Correlation Functions

The simplest correlation function code can be written as:

Code 1. Simple code for a correlation function

```
for(int i=0;i<N1;i++){
  for(int j=0;j<N2;j++){
    double dist = distance_metric(i, j);
    if(dist < mindist || dist >= maxdist){
      continue;
    }

    int ibin = dist_to_bin_index(dist);
    numpairs[ibin]++;
  }
}
```

The only two components that are required to fully specify a correlation function are:

- distance_metric: This specifies how to calculate the separation between the two points. For $\xi(r)$, the separation is simply the *Euclidean* distance between the points
- dist_to_bin_index: This specifies how to map the separation into the histogram bin. Typically, there are ~15–25 bins logarithmically spaced between $\mathcal{R}_{\min}$ and $\mathcal{R}_{\max}$, which span 2–3 orders of magnitude.

In this paper, we will be concentrating on two spatial correlation functions— $\xi(r)$ and $w_p(r_p)$. Consider a pair of distinct points, denoted by the subscripts i and j, with Cartesian positions (x_i, y_i, z_i) and (x_j, y_j, z_j). The separations and the associated constraints (i.e., distance_metric) for $\xi(r)$ and $w_p(r_p)$ are:

$$\xi(r) - \left\{ r := \sqrt{(x_i - x_j)^2 + (y_i - y_j)^2 + (z_i - z_j)^2} < \mathcal{R}_{\max}, \right.$$

$$w_p(r_p) - \begin{cases} r_p := \sqrt{(x_i - x_j)^2 + (y_i - y_j)^2} < \mathcal{R}_{\max} \\ \pi := |z_i - z_j| < \pi_{\max}. \end{cases} \tag{4}$$

Thus, only pairs with $r < \mathcal{R}_{\max}$ add to the histogram for $\xi(r)$; while for $w_p(r_p)$, pairs need to satisfy both conditions $r_p < \mathcal{R}_{\max}$ and $\pi < \pi_{\max}$ before the histogram is updated. Note that the histogram for $w_p(r_p)$ is still only a 1-D histogram based off r_p; the π constraint simply filters out pairs with too large π separation.

So far all we have is the histogram of pair-wise separations for the galaxies. To fully evaluate the correlation function, we also need to evaluate the histogram of pairs for randomly distributed points (see Eq. 2). For simple domain geometry, like a cubic volume with periodic boundary conditions as is common with cosmological simulation data, we can analytically compute the number of random pairs for any histogram bin. Thus, we only need to compute the $N_{DD}(r)$ term in Eq. 2 to calculate $\xi(r)$. A similar technique can be applied to $w_p(r_p)$ as well. Consequently, we only need to compute the $N_{DD}(r)$ (i.e., an auto-correlation) term to calculate both $\xi(r)$ and $w_p(r_p)$.

In real galaxy surveys, the domain geometry is not so simple. In angular extent, the domain is limited by foreground contamination and the sky area the telescope can see from its latitude; in radial extent, it is limited by the faintness of distant galaxies and other complex selection effects. Thus, the $N_{RR}(r)$ and $N_{DR}(r)$ terms must often be computed by pair-counting; this is a major computational expense and is a motivating factor for our development of a fast pair-counting code.

1.2   Partitioning the Space into $\mathcal{R}_{\mathrm{max}}$ Cells

For a given set of N points, a naive implementation of a correlation function would require evaluating all pair-wise separations and hence scale as $\mathcal{O}(N^2)$. However, most correlation functions only require calculating pair-separation up to some maximum separation $\mathcal{R}_{\mathrm{max}}$. If we are only interested in pairs within $\mathcal{R}_{\mathrm{max}}$, then computing the pairwise separation to *all* possible pairs only to discard majority of the computed separations is extremely computationally inefficient. We can create an initial list of potential neighbors and significantly reduce the total number of computations by first partitioning the particles into cells of size at least $\mathcal{R}_{\mathrm{max}}$. This idea of cell lists [6], or chaining meshes [3], is used both in molecular dynamics simulations [4] and smoothed particle hydrodynamics simulations [9].

After depositing the particles into cells of side at least $\mathcal{R}_{\mathrm{max}}$, all possible pairs within $\mathcal{R}_{\mathrm{max}}$ *must* lie within the neighboring cells. In Fig. 1, we show the lattice of side $\mathcal{R}_{\mathrm{max}}$ imposed on the Poisson distributed red points. For any given query point (in blue), we first locate the target cell and then we immediately know all potential cells that may contain pairs. However, this lattice implementation approximates the volume of a sphere of radius $\mathcal{R}_{\mathrm{max}}$ by that of a cube with side $3 \times \mathcal{R}_{\mathrm{max}}$. Thus, if we compute all possible pair-separations, then only 16% of the separations will be within $\mathcal{R}_{\mathrm{max}}$; the remaining 84% will be spurious [2]. In Fig. 2, we show that sub-dividing the cells further reduces the effective search volume. Sub-dividing the cells into size $\mathcal{R}_{\mathrm{max}}/2$, the spurious calculations drop to $\sim$63% [2]. Continuing to sub-divide further reduces the spurious calculations even more, but the overhead of searching over many more neighboring cells starts to dominate. In our experience with Corrfunc, we have found that bin sizes in the vicinity of $\mathcal{R}_{\mathrm{max}}/2$ produce the fastest run-times for a broad range of use-cases.

2   Overview of Corrfunc

2.1   Optimization Design

Corrfunc provides a variety of high-performance, OpenMP parallel, user-friendly correlation function codes. We have presented Corrfunc in [8] but to make this

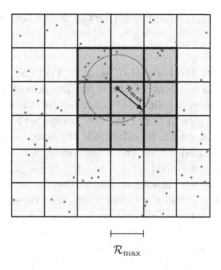

$\mathcal{R}_{\mathrm{max}}$

Fig. 1. Partitioning the space to speed up the search for any potential pair within $\mathcal{R}_{\mathrm{max}}$. The distribution of red points is gridded up on a lattice with cell-size at least $\mathcal{R}_{\mathrm{max}}$. For any blue query point, all possible pairs involving the red points *must* lie within the 9 neighboring cells (dark gray shaded cells). With a similar lattice structure in 3 dimensions, we approximate a sphere of volume $\frac{4}{3}\pi\mathcal{R}_{\mathrm{max}}^3$ with a cube of volume $27\mathcal{R}_{\mathrm{max}}^3$. Figure adapted from [8]. (Color figure online)

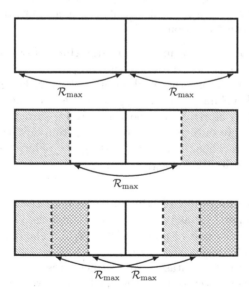

Fig. 2. Refining the cell-size reduces the search volume. Particles in the shaded regions are separated by more than $\mathcal{R}_{\mathrm{max}}$ and can not have a pair. Compared to the top panel, the middle and lower panels need to inspect a smaller search volume. Figure adapted from [8]. (Color figure online)

paper self-contained, we will briefly describe the design and optimizations implemented in `Corrfunc`.

Creating 3D Cells to Reduce the Search Volume. As we discussed in Sect. 1.2, the computational cost of searching for potential neighbors can be reduced by dividing the space into 3D cells. Given two sets of positions, the correlation function routines in `Corrfunc` first computes a bounding box for the two datasets. The second step is to sub-divide the space into 3D cells such that all possible pairs are located within the neighboring cells (see Fig. 1). However, for an optimal grid size, we need to account for the separation in the specific correlation function. As we showed in Eq. 4, the $\xi(r)$ calculation only needs pairs that satisfy $r < \mathcal{R}_{\max}$ and correspondingly the grid-size is some fraction of $\mathcal{R}_{\max}$. For $w_p(r_p)$, we need two different separations – r_p and π, where r_p is the separation between a pair of points in the X-Y plane, and π is the separation along the Z axis. Therefore, the optimal grid-size is some fraction of $\mathcal{R}_{\max}$ in both X and Y axes, and $\pi_{\max}$ along the Z axes. We combine the two cases into $\pi < \pi_{\max}$, with the understanding that $\pi_{\max} = \mathcal{R}_{\max}$ for $\xi(r)$ calculations.

Improving Cache Utilization. Within each cell, the particle positions are stored as a Structure-of-Array (SoA) variable. The individual X, Y, Z positions are copied from the input arrays and duplicated within dedicated pointers in the SoA cell-array. Since we can load in the positions from the SoA cell-array directly into vector registers without any shuffle operations, the SoA operation is very conducive to vectorization.

Reducing the Search Volume by Sorting the z Positions. With some appropriate sub-divisions, we can now locate all possible pairs that satisfy the separation constraints among the neighboring cell pairs. For $\xi(r)$ calculations, the spherical search volume of $4/3\pi\mathcal{R}_{\max}^3$ is then approximated with $27\mathcal{R}_{\max}^3$. The particle positions stored in the SoA are always sorted along the Z axis. With such a sorting, we only need to seek $\pm\pi_{\max}$ from any particle position to find all possible pairs. Thus, with the Z-sorting, we reduce the search volume along the Z axis from $3\pi_{\max}$ to $2\pi_{\max}$.

Reducing the Number of Cell Pairs. Once both the datasets have been gridded up and the particles assigned to cells, we associate all possible pairs of cells that may contain a pair of points within $\mathcal{R}_{\max}$. The fundamental unit of work within `Corrfunc` involve such pairs of cells.

For cases where the two datasets are distinct (cross-correlations), there are no symmetry conditions to exploit. However, when the two datasets are identical (auto-correlations), we can take advantage of symmetry. Only unique pairs of cells need to calculated, and as long as we double the total number of pairs found at the end, we will still have the correct number of pairs. Both $\xi(r)$ and $w_p(r_p)$ are auto-correlations and benefit from this optimization.

2.2   Computing the Minimum Possible Separation

After culling for cell-pairs based on symmetry, we are left with cell-pairs that are within $\mathcal{R}_{\max}$ along any one dimension, but might still be too far apart when the full 3D separation is considered. To remove such cell-pairs, we need to compute the minimum possible separation between these two cells. Based on the linear offset between the cell-pairs along each dimension, we know the minimum possible separations, Δ_X, Δ_Y and Δ_Z along each axis. However, these quantities only capture the extent of the individual cells and do not reflect the actual positions of the particles within the cell. Therefore, we also store the bounding box info for each cell. With the bounding box, we can then compute the minimum possible separation between the two cells by simply taking the difference of the bounding axes along each dimension and then using Eq. 4. If the minimum possible separation is larger than $\mathcal{R}_{\max}$, then there *can not* be any valid pairs between the particles in the two cells and we reject that cell-pair.

If a cell-pair passes this check, then there *may* exist at least one valid pair between the cells. So far the Δ_X and related quantities only reflect the minimum possible separation between the cell-edges. Δ_X could really reflect the minimum separation between *any pair* of particles. Since we have the bounding box info for the secondary cell, we increase each one of the three Δ_X quantities by the separation between the secondary bounding box and the nearest secondary cell-edge. If most of the secondary particles are concentrated towards the center of the secondary cell, then we would increase Δ_X by a large amount and correspondingly prune a larger chunk of the secondary particles.

Late-Entry and Early-Exit from the j-loop. For any pair of cells, we know the minimum possible particle separation along each of the X, Y and Z axes – Δ_x, Δ_y and Δ_z respectively. We also store the positions for the X, Y and Z edges of the primary cell nearest to the secondary cell – X_{edge}, Y_{edge} and Z_{edge} respectively. Since the minimum possible separation (between any particle pairs) along X and Y axes is Δ_x and Δ_y, and the maximum total separation is $\mathcal{R}_{\max}$, the maximum possible $dz := (z_i - z_j)$ that can satisfy $r < \mathcal{R}_{\max}$:

$$dz_{\max,\text{all}} = SQRT(\mathcal{R}_{\max}^2 - \Delta_X^2 - \Delta_Y^2), \qquad (5)$$

This $dz_{\max,\text{all}}$ only makes sense for $\xi(r)$; for $w_p(r_p)$ calculations $dz_{\max,\text{all}}$ equals $\pi_{\max}$.

In addition, we can also compute the minimum possible separation between a given primary particle and *any* secondary particle. We can make an improved estimate for the minimum separation between the i'th primary particle and any secondary particle by using the X and Y positions of the primary particle. For every cell-pair we can then compute two conditions Therefore, we can compute the minimum possible

$$dx_{i,\min} = \Delta_X + |(x_i - X_{edge})|, \qquad (6)$$
$$dy_{i,\min} = \Delta_Y + |(y_i - Y_{edge})|, \qquad (7)$$

$$dz_{i,\max} = \sqrt{\mathcal{R}_{\max}^2 - dx_{i,\min}^2 - dy_{i,\min}^2} \qquad (8)$$

Recall that the z values in are sorted in increasing order, i.e., $z_j \leq z_{j+1} \leq z_{j+2}, ...$, as well as $z_i \leq z_{i+1} \leq z_{i+2}, ...$ If we define $dz_{ji} := z_j - z_i$, then the dz values are also in increasing order for a fixed value of i. Therefore, if any particle in the second dataset has $dz_{ji} > dz_{i,\max}$, *all* future particles from the second data also must have $dz > dz_{i,\max}$. When we encounter such a j particle, we terminate the j-loop and continue on with the next iteration of the outer i-loop.

Since the dz_{ji} values are effectively sorted in increasing order, for a given i, the smallest value of dz_{ij} (note flipped subscripts) will occur for the final j-th particle. Since the z positions in the first dataset are also sorted in increasing order, therefore $dz_{ij} \leq dz_{(i+1)j} \leq dz_{(i+2)j}...$ Thus, $dz_{i(N2-1)}$ is also the smallest possible value for all remaining pairs between the two datasets. Therefore, if $dz_{i(N2-1)}$ exceeds $dz_{\max,\mathrm{all}}$, no further pairs are possible and we can exit the outer i-loop altogether.

For any i-th particle to have a pair in the second dataset, the condition $dz_{ji} < |\min(\pi_{\max}, dz_{i,\max})|$ must be met. Therefore if $dz_{ji} \geq dz_{i,\max}$, there can not be any possible pair between this i-th particle and *any* j particles. However, a different particle from the first dataset might still be a valid pair with the remaining particles in the second dataset. Therefore, we simply continue on with the next iteration of the i-loop.

Since the z positions are sorted, we continue to loop over the j particles, until we find a j such that $dz_{ji} > -dz_{i,\max}$. This j marks the beginning particle for calculating pairwise separations.

Code 2. Late Entry and early exit condition

```
const DOUBLE *zstart = z2;
const DOUBLE *zend = z2 + N2;
DOUBLE dz_max_all = SQRT(rmax^2
                         - \Delta_X^2
                         - \Delta_Y^2);
for(int64_t i=0;i<N1;i++) {
  const DOUBLE xpos = *x1++;
  const DOUBLE ypos = *y1++;
  const DOUBLE zpos = *z1++;

  DOUBLE this_dz = *z2 - zpos;
  if(this_dz >= dz_max_all) continue;

  DOUBLE dx = \Delta_X > 0 ?
              ABS(\Delta_X) + ABS(xpos - X_edge):0;
  DOUBLE dy = \Delta_Y > 0 ?
              ABS(\Delta_Y) + ABS(ypos - Y_edge):0;
  DOUBLE dz = \Delta_Z > 0 ?
              ABS(\Delta_Z) + ABS(zpos - Z_edge):0;
```

```
DOUBLE sqr_sep = dx^2 + dy^2 + dz^2;
if(sqr_sep >= rmax^2) continue;
DOUBLE max_dz = SQRT(rmax^2 - dx^2 - dy^2);

while( (*z2 - zpos) <= -dz_max_all) {
  z2++;
}
if(z2 == zend) break;

int64_t j = z2 - zstart;
```

Vector Intrinsics in Existing SIMD Kernels. In [8], we presented the dedicated AVX and SSE kernels. These kernels operate on cell pairs, finding all possible pairs between the two cells and updating the histogram appropriately. Both the AVX and SSE kernels have an associated header file each that maps C-macros to the correct underlying intrinsic for both double and single precision floats. With such an approach, the same lines of (pseudo-)intrinsics in the SIMD kernels can be seamlessly used for both single and double precision floats.

We vectorize the j-loop over the second set of points and process particles in chunks of SIMDLEN; where SIMDLEN is 8 and 4 for single-precision AVX and SSE respectively. For double precision calculations, SIMDLEN is halved and equals 4 and 2 for AVX and SSE respectively.

Immediately following from Code 2, we can start processing pairs of particles with SIMD intrinsics.

Code 3. The loop over secondary particles in SIMD kernels

```
int64_t j = z2 - zstart;
DOUBLE *localz2 = z2;
DOUBLE *localx2 = x2 + j;
DOUBLE *localy2 = y2 + j;
SIMD_DOUBLE simd_xpos = SIMD_SPLAT(xpos);
SIMD_DOUBLE simd_ypos = SIMD_SPLAT(ypos);
SIMD_DOUBLE simd_zpos = SIMD_SPLAT(zpos);

SIMD_DOUBLE simd_sqr_rmax = SIMD_SPLAT(rmax^2);
SIMD_DOUBLE simd_sqr_rmin = SIMD_SPLAT(rmin^2);

for(;j<=(N2 - SIMDLEN);j+=SIMDLEN) {
  SIMD_DOUBLE simd_x2 = SIMD_LOAD(localx2);
  SIMD_DOUBLE simd_y2 = SIMD_LOAD(localy2);
  SIMD_DOUBLE simd_z2 = SIMD_LOAD(localz2);

  localx2 += SIMD_LEN;
  localy2 += SIMD_LEN;
  localz2 += SIMD_LEN;
```

```
SIMD_DOUBLE dx = SIMD_SUB(simd_x2 - simd_xpos);
SIMD_DOUBLE dy = SIMD_SUB(simd_y2 - simd_ypos);
SIMD_DOUBLE dz = SIMD_SUB(simd_z2 - simd_zpos);

if( ALL(dz <= -max_dz) ) continue;
if( ANY(dz >= max_dz) ) j = N2;

SIMD_DOUBLE rp2 = SIMD_ADD(SIMD_MUL(dx, dx),
                           SIMD_MUL(dy, dy));
SIMD_DOUBLE r2 = SIMD_ADD(rp2,
                          SIMD_MUL(dz, dz));

SIMD_MASK rmax_pairs = SIMD_CMP_LT(r2, sqr_rmax);
SIMD_MASK rmin_pairs = SIMD_CMP_GE(r2, sqr_rmin);
SIMD_MASK pairs_left = SIMD_AND(rmax_pairs,
                               rmin_pairs);
if( NONE(pairs_left) ) continue;

/* histogram update here */
}

for(;j<N2; j++) { /* remainder loop */
```

Since we can only process multiples of SIMDLEN with the SIMD intrinsics, we need an additional remainder loop to process any remaining particles in the second dataset.

Once we have a set of SIMD vectors, calculating the separations is trivial. Note that we avoid the expensive sqrt operation in Eq. 4 and always perform comparisons with squared separations. Once we have the (squared) separations, we can create vector masks for separations that satisfy the conditions in Eq. 4. If no particles satisfy the distance constraints, then we continue to process the next SIMDLEN chunk. If there are particles that do satisfy all distance criteria, then the histogram needs to be updated.

Updating the Histogram of Pair-Counts. Within the SIMD kernels, we have the array containing the values of the lower and upper edges of the histogram bins. To update the histogram, we need to first ascertain which bin any given r falls into. The simplest way to locate the bin is to loop through the bins, and stop when r is within the bin-edges. Recall that we avoid computing $r := \sqrt{r^2}$, so the comparison is $r_{low}^2 \leq r^2 < r_{hi}^2$. However, we can take advantage of how the typical bins are spaced and perform the histogram update faster.

Code 4. Histogram Update in SIMD kernels

```
for(int kbin=nbin-1;kbin>=1;kbin--) {
    SIMD_DOUBLE m1 = SIMD_CMP_GE(r2, rupp_sqr[kbin-1]);
```

```
        SIMD_MASK bin_mask = SIMD_AND(m1, pairs_left);
        npairs[kbin] += POPCNT(SIMD_TEST(bin_mask));
        pairs_left = SIMD_CMP_LT(r2, rupp_sqr[kbin-1]);
        if( NONE(pairs_left) ) break;
}
```

Typically the histogram bins are logarithmically spaced, and consequently, the outer bins encompass a much larger volume than the inner bins. Therefore, many more pairs of points are likely to fall in the outer bins than the inner ones. Following [1], we loop backwards through the histogram bins (see Code 4). Within the SIMD kernels, we create a mask that evaluates to 'true' separations that fell within a bin. We then run a hardware popcnt operation to count the number of bits set and update that particular histogram bin. This iteration over the histogram stops once we have accounted for all valid separations.

2.3   Overview of AVX512F

AVX512 is the latest generation of instruction set architecture supported on both the Intel SkyLake-SP, Skylake-X and the Xeon Phi x2000 (Knights Landing) processors. AVX512 expands the vector length to 512-bytes (compared to the 256-bytes in AVX) and introduces an additional mask variable type. Every instruction now comes with a masked variety where some elements can be masked out and alternate values specified for those masked-out lanes. The dedicated mask variable type can be directly cast into an uint16_t.[1]

Since AVX512 is composed of several distinct instruction sets, both current and upcoming, we have only targeted the specific subset – AVX512-Foundation (AVX512F). AVX512F is meant to be supported by all current and future processors with AVX512 support[2].

2.4   AVX512F Kernel Implementation

Within the AVX512F kernel, we employ the same late-entry and early-exit conditions discussed in Sect. 2.2. In this subsection, we will describe the AVX512F kernel once the first possible particle in the j-loop is identified.

The masked operations are quite handy when coding up the AVX512F kernel. For instance, typically the array lengths are not an exact multiple of the SIMD vector length. Therefore, at the end of each vectorized loop, there is always a 'remainder' loop (see Code 3) to process the elements that were left over. With the masked operations in AVX512F, we can pad out the 'remainder' points to be an exact SIMD vector length; and set the mask for these padded points as 'false' (see Code 5). All of the subsequent processing, including the 'load' from memory, then uses this mask as one of the operands. Since there is no longer

---

[1] For double precision calculations, the upper 8 bits of the mask are identically set to 0.

[2] AVX512CD is meant to allow vectorization of histogram updates but our attempts at automatic vectorization have proved futile so far.

any 'remainder-loop', the Corrfunc AVX512F kernels are automatically more compact.

Code 5. The j-loop in AVX512F kernels

```
const uint16_t masks_left_float [] =
{
  0xFFFF,
  0x0001, 0x0003, 0x0007, 0x000F,
  0x001F, 0x003F, 0x007F, 0x00FF,
  0x01FF, 0x03FF, 0x07FF, 0x0FFF,
  0x1FFF, 0x3FFF, 0x7FFF
};

const uint8_t masks_left_double [] =
{
  0xFF,
  0x01,0x03,0x07,0x0F,
  0x1F,0x3F,0x7F
};

int64_t n_off = z2 - zstart;
int64_t Nleft = N2 - n_off;
DOUBLE *localz2 = z2;
DOUBLE *localx2 = x2 + n_off;
DOUBLE *localy2 = y2 + n_off;
for(int64_t j=0;j<Nleft;j+=AVX512_NVEC) {
  AVX512_MASK mask_left = (Nleft - j) >= SIMDLEN ?
  masks_left_DOUBLE[0]:masks_left_DOUBLE[Nleft-j];
  ...
}
```

With such a masked load, we can completely avoid the 'remainder' loop. We simply continue to update the mask variable – mask_left – while processing the SIMDLEN separations per iteration of the j-loop. In other words, we used masked comparisons, where the input mask already contains the mask_left.

Most of the remaining sections of the AVX512F kernel follows similarly to the previous kernels. The two significant updates in the AVX512F kernels are that we have used the FMA operations where possible, and instead of the hardware popcnt instruction, we have used a pre-computed array containing the number of bits set.

3   Results

In this section we will show the performance results from the newest AVX512F kernel and compare to the previous AVX, SSE and Fallback kernels within Corrfunc. To run the benchmarks in Sects. 3.1 and 3.2, we have used the

Intel C compiler suite 2018 (icc/2018.1.163) on a dedicated node with the Intel Skylake 6140 cpus at the OzSTAR supercomputing Centre (https://supercomputing.swin.edu.au/ozstar/). `Corrfunc` was compiled with the compilation flag `-O3 -xhost -axCORE-AVX512 -qopenmp`. We used the git commit `7b698823af216f39331ffdf46288de57e554ad06` to run these benchmarks.

To run the benchmarks in Sect. 3.3, we used the Intel C compiler (2017) with the same compiler flags. The hardware setup was a dual socket machine with two Intel Xeon Gold 6132 @ 2.60 GHz, for 28 threads total.

3.1   Comparing the Performance with Sub-divided Cells

We showed in Sect. 1.2 that if we keep the cell sizes at $\mathcal{R}_{\max}$, then only 16% of the pairs computed are likely to be necessary. Within `Corrfunc`, we have the runtime option of refining the cell-size further. There are 3 "bin refinement factors" corresponding to each of the X, Y and Z axes. These bin refinement factors dictate how many further sub-divisions of the initial $\mathcal{R}_{\max}$ cell are made. Based on past experience, refining along the Z axis only degrades performance; therefore, we have fixed the Z refinement at 1 and only allowed the refinements to vary along the X and Y axes. In Fig. 3, we show how reducing the cell-size impacts the total runtime for a $\xi(r)$ calculation, with $\mathcal{R}_{\max} = 25$ in a periodic box of side 420. We let the X and Y bin refinement factors to vary between 1 and 3. Every combination of (m, n) represents cell-sizes of $(dx, dy) \gtrsim (\mathcal{R}_{\max}/m, \mathcal{R}_{\max}/n)$. In Fig. 3 we see that `AVX512F` kernel is by far the fastest, followed by the `AVX`, the `SSE` and the `Fallback` kernels. This relative ordering of the kernels is in keeping with the relative ordering of the vector register sizes.

Within each kernel group, the coarsest sub-division—$(1, 1)$—is the slowest with the performance improving with higher bin refinement factors. However, all kernels are slower for bin refinements of $(3, 3)$ indicating that the overhead of looping over neighbor cells dominates over the reduction in the search volume from the bin refinements (see Fig. 2). The improvement in the runtime for the `Fallback` kernel is drastic—$\sim$50% faster in moving from $(1, 1)$ to $(2, 3)$. The `SIMD` kernels also show variations in the runtime with different bin refinement factors but the scatter seems to reduce with wider vector registers. For instance, the `AVX512F` kernels show the least variation in runtime with the bin refinement factors while the `SSE` kernels show the largest variation.

Within `Corrfunc`, we simply set the default bin refinement factor to $(2, 2, 1)$ and recommend that the user experiment with various refinement factors to find out what produces the fastest code for their use-case. With the new `AVX512F` kernel, the same default bin refinement factors continue to be the fastest option. As we showed in Fig. 2, since the search volume reduces with higher bin refinement factors, we do expect a reduction in runtime. However, the exact speedup obtained is likely to be strongly dependent on $\mathcal{R}_{\max}$ and the number density of the particles. Exploring this dependence of the speedup on $\mathcal{R}_{\max}$ and the particle load and automatically setting the `bin refinement factors` to close-to-optimal values would be a great improvement to the `Corrfunc` package.

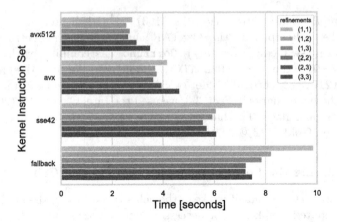

Fig. 3. How sub-dividing the cells into sizes smaller than $\mathcal{R}_{\max}$ improves runtime performance. In this figure, the colors represent different combinations of the X and Y cell sizes (dx and dy). The individual (m, n) in the figure represent (dx, dy) $\gtrsim$ ($\mathcal{R}_{\max}/m, \mathcal{R}_{\max}/n$) For example, (1, 1) is the case where (dx, dy) $\gtrsim \mathcal{R}_{\max}$, (1, 2) is where $dx \gtrsim \mathcal{R}_{\max}, dy \gtrsim \mathcal{R}_{\max}/2$ and so on. The AVX512F kernels are the fastest, followed by the AVX, the SSE and the Fallback kernels. There is variation of up to 50% in runtime (for the Fallback case) for different bin refine factors; the variation in runtime is less pronounced (~20%) in the SIMD kernels. Thus, choosing an optimal cell-size is an important aspect of performance. (Color figure online)

3.2   Comparing the Performance with Bounding Box Optimizations

In Sect. 2.2, we discussed how we maintain a bounding box for every cell. After computing the minimum possible separation based on the bounding box, we can then reject any cell-pair that can not contain a particle pair within $\mathcal{R}_{\max}$. In addition, for every primary particle, we can compute the minimum possible separation to any secondary particle. If this minimum separation is larger than $\mathcal{R}_{\max}$, then we simply continue with the next primary particle. In Fig. 4 we show the performance improvement based on the minimum separation calculations. We can see that the performance improvement is typically in the 5–10% range, with the latest instruction sets showing the smallest improvement. Since the minimum separation calculation is done in scalar mode, that optimization means more time is spent in the scalar section of the SIMD kernel and consequently the kernels with the widest vector registers show the smallest improvement. In addition, we also see that the improvement generally reduces as the number of sub-divisions increases. This is most likely a combination of two effects – (i) increased runtime overhead for processing larger number of neighbor cells, and (ii) overall lower amount of computation per cell pair (due to smaller number of particles per cell) means the potential work avoided with the minimum separation calculation is lower.

The dataset we have used for the benchmark contains a modest 1.2 million galaxies. It is quite likely that the minimum separation optimization will have a larger impact for larger dataset (or equivalently, a larger $\mathcal{R}_{max}$).

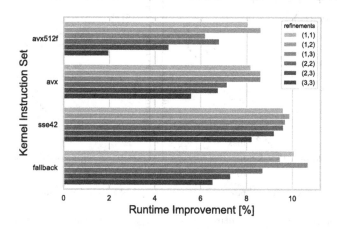

Fig. 4. How the runtime changes for each SIMD kernel by calculating the minimum separation between cell-pairs, as well as the minimum separation for a primary particle and all remaining particles in the secondary cell (see Sect. 2.2). The colors show the different refinements (see Sects. 1.2 and 3.1). The improvement ranges from few% to ~10% across all the SIMD kernels; however, the performance improvement seems to reduce when there are a larger number of sub-divisions. (Color figure online)

3.3 Comparing the Performance of the SIMD Kernels

In the preceding section we saw that the AVX512F kernels in $\xi(r)$ are the fastest for a for a fixed value of $\mathcal{R}_{max}$. We also wish to validate that AVX512F performs well for a broad range of $\mathcal{R}_{max}$. Typical values of $\mathcal{R}_{max}$ range from few percent to 25% of the periodic box size, so we explore this range in our tests. In the following, the box size of the test dataset is 420; we show performance for $\mathcal{R}_{max}$ values between 10 and 100.

In this section, we will compare the performance of the four SIMD kernels for a range of $\mathcal{R}_{max}$ values, with the calculations being done in double precision. For $\xi(r)$, increasing $\mathcal{R}_{max}$ means increasing the search volume as $\mathcal{R}_{max}^3$. For $w_p(r_p)$, we have fixed $\pi_{max} = \mathcal{R}_{max}$; hence, increasing $\mathcal{R}_{max}$ also increases the search volume by $\mathcal{R}_{max}^2 \times \pi_{max} = \mathcal{R}_{max}^3$. Thus, in both cases we expect an asymptotic $\mathcal{R}_{max}^3$ runtime scaling.

In Fig. 5, we show how the various kernel run-times scale. We see the expected $\mathcal{R}_{max}^3$ behavior at large $\mathcal{R}_{max}$, with the AVX512F kernels being the fastest for reasonably large $\mathcal{R}_{max}$. At the lowest $\mathcal{R}_{max}$ values, each cell contains only a small

number of particles and it is likely that there is not sufficient computational work
to keep the wider vector registers full.[3]

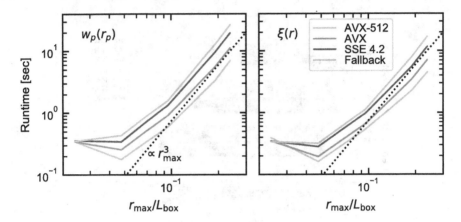

Fig. 5. Correlation function runtime versus $\mathcal{R}_{\max}$. For the $w_p(r_p)$ calculations (left
panel), we have set $\pi_{\max} := \mathcal{R}_{\max}$. The effective search volume is then either that of a
sphere, $4/3\pi\mathcal{R}_{\max}^3$ for $\xi(r)$ or a cylinder $\pi\mathcal{R}_{\max}^2\pi_{\max} = \pi\mathcal{R}_{\max}^3$, since $\pi_{\max} = \mathcal{R}_{\max}$ for
this test. Thus, in both the $\xi(r)$ and $w_p(r_p)$ cases, the search volume scales as $\mathcal{R}_{\max}^3$ and
correspondingly both the correlation functions scale accordingly. As we summarized in
Table 1, we find that the AVX512F kernels are faster by $\sim 3.9\times$ relative to the Fallback
kernel, and $\sim 1.6\times$ relative to the AVX kernel.

Now that we have seen the raw performance, let us compare the speedups
obtained by the vectorized kernels relative to the Fallback kernel which contains
no explicit SIMD instructions. Since the calculations are done in double precision,
a priori we expect a theoretical maximum of $8\times, 4\times, 2\times$ speedup for the AVX512F,
AVX and SSE kernels, assuming the compiler is not able to automatically generate
any vectorized instructions. Even in the case that the compiler is able to do so,
this test will measure how much more efficient our vector implementation is than
the compiler's.

In Table 1 we show the speedup obtained with the various SIMD kernels relative to the Fallback kernel for a range of values for $\mathcal{R}_{\max}$. We see that for
$\mathcal{R}_{\max} = 10$, there is essentially no performance boost from the vectorized ker-
nels. Once $\mathcal{R}_{\max}$ is $\gtrsim 80$, the speedup seems to stabilize at $\sim 3.8\times, 2.3\times, 1.3\times$
for the AVX512F, AVX and the SSE kernels respectively. These achieved speedups
are within a factor of 2 of the theoretical maximum speedup. More interestingly,
the AVX512F is $1.6\times$ faster than the AVX kernels, compared to the theoretical
maximum of $2\times$ speedup from the wider vector registers. We also use the FMA
operations in AVX512F kernels, which also adds to the potential speedup.

---

[3] A low $\mathcal{R}_{\max}$ is potentially a case where the bin refinement factors need to be set to
$(1, 1, 1)$ to boost the particle occupancy in the cells.

Table 1. Speedup from the SIMD kernels relative to the Fallback kernel as a function of $\mathcal{R}_{max}$. For $w_p(r_p)$ calculations, we have set $\pi_{max} = \mathcal{R}_{max}$. All of these calculations are done with a simulation box of periodic size 420.0.

$\mathcal{R}_{max}$	$w_p(r_p)$				$\xi(r)$			
	AVX512F	AVX	SSE	Fallback	AVX512F	AVX	SSE	Fallback
10.0	1.1×	1.0×	1.0×	1.0×	1.0×	1.0×	0.9×	1.0×
20.0	2.7×	1.8×	1.3×	1.0×	2.2×	1.8×	1.1×	1.0×
40.0	3.0×	1.8×	1.2×	1.0×	2.4×	1.9×	1.2×	1.0×
80.0	3.9×	2.3×	1.3×	1.0×	3.6×	2.3×	1.4×	1.0×
100.0	3.8×	2.4×	1.4×	1.0×	3.8×	2.4×	1.5×	1.0×

4   Conclusions

In this paper, we have presented AVX512F kernels for calculating correlation functions within the open-source package Corrfunc. These AVX512F kernels have been manually coded with vector intrinsics and make extensive use of masked operations to compute the separations and then update the histogram of pair-counts. The AVX512F kernels show a typical speedup for ∼3.8× relative to the compiler-generated code within the Fallback kernel. The speedup is ∼1.6× relative to the AVX kernel and compares very well to the theoretical maximum of 2×. In addition, by efficiently pruning pairs that have separations larger than $\mathcal{R}_{max}$, we gained up to a 10% speedup. This paper and [8] highlight the importance of combining domain knowledge, efficient algorithms, and dedicated vector intrinsics for complex calculations. Such combinations are particularly powerful when the underlying problem is difficult for the compiler to efficiently vectorize, as is the case for Corrfunc.

Acknowledgements. MS was primarily supported by NSF Career Award (AST-1151650) during main Corrfunc design and development. MS was also supported by the by the Australian Research Council Laureate Fellowship (FL110100072) awarded to Stuart Wyithe and by funds for the Theoretical Astrophysical Observatory (TAO). TAO is part of the All-Sky Virtual Observatory and is funded and supported by Astronomy Australia Limited, Swinburne University of Technology, and the Australian Government. The latter is provided though the Commonwealth's Education Investment Fund and National Collaborative Research Infrastructure Strategy (NCRIS), particularly the National eResearch Collaboration Tools and Resources (NeCTAR) project. Parts of this research were conducted by the Australian Research Council Centre of Excellence for All Sky Astrophysics in 3 Dimensions (ASTRO 3D), through project number CE170100013.

References

1. Chhugani, J., et al.: Billion-particle SIMD-friendly two-point correlation on large-scale HPC cluster systems. In: Proceedings of the International Conference on High Performance Computing, Networking, Storage and Analysis, SC 2012, pp. 1:1–1:11. IEEE Computer Society Press, Los Alamitos (2012). http://dl.acm.org/citation. cfm?id=2388996.2388998
2. Gonnet, P.: A simple algorithm to accelerate the computation of non-bonded interactions in cell-based molecular dynamics simulations. J. Comput. Chem. **28**(2), 570–573 (2007). https://doi.org/10.1002/jcc.20563. https://onlinelibrary.wiley.com/doi/abs/10.1002/jcc.20563
3. Hockney, R., Goel, S., Eastwood, J.: Quiet high-resolution computer models of a plasma. J. Comput. Phys. **14**(2), 148–158 (1974). https://doi.org/10.1016/0021-9991(74)90010-2. http://www.sciencedirect.com/science/article/pii/0021999174900102
4. Lindahl, E., Hess, B., van der Spoel, D.: GROMACS 3.0: a package for molecular simulation and trajectory analysis. Mol. Model. Annu. **7**, 306–317 (2001). https://doi.org/10.1007/s008940100045. https://link.springer.com/article/10.1007/s008940100045
5. Peebles, P.J.E.: The Large-Scale Structure of the Universe. Princeton University Press, Princeton (1980)
6. Quentrec, B., Brot, C.: New method for searching for neighbors in molecular dynamics computations. J. Comput. Phys. **13**(3), 430–432 (1973). https://doi.org/10.1016/0021-9991(73)90046-6. http://www.sciencedirect.com/science/article/pii/0021999173900466
7. Sinha, M., Berlind, A.A., McBride, C.K., Scoccimarro, R., Piscionere, J.A., Wibking, B.D.: Towards accurate modelling of galaxy clustering on small scales: testing the standard ΛCDM + halo model. MNRAS **478**, 1042–1064 (2018). https://doi.org/10.1093/mnras/sty967
8. Sinha, M., Lehman, G.: Corrfunc—a suite of blazing fast correlation functions on the CPU. MNRAS (2019). (Submitted to MNRAS)
9. Willis, J.S., Schaller, M., Gonnet, P., Bower, R.G., Draper, P.W.: An efficient SIMD implementation of pseudo-Verlet lists for neighbour interactions in particle-based codes. ArXiv e-prints, April 2018

High Level File System and Parallel I/O Optimization of DNS Code

Bipin Kumar[1]([⊠]) [ORCID], Nachiket Manapragada[2], and Neethi Suresh[1]

[1] Indian Institute of Tropical Meteorology,
Dr. Homi Bhabha Road, Pashan, Pune 411008, India
bipink@tropmet.res.in
[2] Cray Supercomputers (India) Pvt Ltd.,
Level 4, Parabhavi Tech Park Baner, Pune 411045, India

Abstract. The representation of clouds and convection has an enormous impact on simulation of the climate system. Clouds play key role in behavior of weather elements. They have a huge impact on earth radiation budget system, water and energy cycle and hence controlling the climate. There are lot of biases in current atmospheric general circulation models because of inadequate understanding of micro-physical processes and the hydrodynamics in clouds. For improving the models, small scale simulation such as Direct Numerical Simulation (DNS) is required which solves equations without any assumptions. DNS is very complex and requires huge amount of computational resources. These simulations are memory intensive as well as consuming large space for I/O. Writing huge files at run-time is a challenging task and requires optimization in parallel I/O. This study presents different types of optimization for Lustre file system and advanced vector extension 2. The optimization has improved the code by reducing total simulation time significantly.

Keywords: DNS · Parallel I/O optimization · Striping ·
NUMA optimization · IOBUF optimization

1 Introduction

The significance of turbulent entrainment in cumulus clouds and its impact on droplet concentration was brought to light by Stommel [9] in his paper. Throughout the entire life cycle of cloud, the entrainment of clear air and its mixing with cloudy air takes place. Such mixings in warm clouds contains highly turbulent flows across spatial and temporal scales of many orders of magnitude and these complex microphysical processes involve mass and heat transfer and phase change. Because of simulation limitations these processes are still not understood completely.

Earlier studies on entrainment and mixing in clouds include Direct Numerical Simulations (DNS) which relies on numerical simulations in 3-D focusing on

Supported by Ministry of Earth Science Government of India.

A. Majumdar and R. Arora (Eds.): SCEC 2018, CCIS 964, pp. 21–31, 2019.
https://doi.org/10.1007/978-981-13-7729-7_2

cloud microstructure. Vaillancourt et al. [11,12] studied early stage diffusional growth of droplets due to adiabatic rising of parcel of moist air in cloud core. For better understanding of droplet dynamics they combined the Lagrangian approach with the Eulerian frame of relevant turbulent fields (water vapor mixing ratio, temperature, velocity). The Eulerian phase is used for solving the turbulent flow fields and Lagrangian phase is used for tracking droplet trajectories.

The 3D cloud dynamics simulation of this sort is not only a highly compute intensive task but also has huge memory requirement. Various strategies of developing parallel algorithms to take advantage of modern super computers with multicore processors have been attempted. Heimsund and Espedal [2] discussed one such strategy for parallelization of Eulerian-Lagrangian localized adjoint method for both distributed and shared memory. Herrmann [3] documented a method using a parallel algorithm for Eulerian-Lagrangian for two phase fluid flow.

This paper explores Eulerian part of DNS code and exploits the hardware and software stack of Cray XC40 machine for optimization. The paper is organized as follows. Next sections describe the mathematical model for fluid flow as well as droplet movement. Optimization methodologies are presented in Sect. 3. Section 4 contains the description of data used. Subsequent sections provides results and discussion. Conclusion and outlook of this work is described in last section.

2   Mathematical Model

The DNS code used this study solve 3D turbulent flow fields. The governing equations for turbulent flow as well as droplet growth and movement are taken from [1,6]. The turbulent fluid flow equations, namely the velocity field $\mathbf{u}$, the vapor mixing ratio $\mathbf{q_v}$ field and the temperature field $\mathbf{T}$, can be written as follows

$$\nabla \cdot \mathbf{u} = 0, \tag{1}$$

$$\partial_t \mathbf{u} + (\mathbf{u} \cdot \nabla)\mathbf{u} = -\frac{1}{\rho_0}\nabla p + \nu\nabla^2\mathbf{u} + B\mathbf{e}_z + \mathbf{f}_{LS}, \tag{2}$$

$$\partial_t T + \mathbf{u} \cdot \nabla T = \kappa\nabla^2 T + \frac{L}{c_p}C_d, \tag{3}$$

$$\partial_t q_v + \mathbf{u} \cdot \nabla q_v = D\nabla^2 q_v - C_d. \tag{4}$$

The reference density is the dry air density. The buoyancy term in the momentum equation is defined as

$$B = g\left[\frac{T'}{\langle T \rangle} + \varepsilon q'_v - q_l\right]. \tag{5}$$

Here, ν is the kinematic viscosity of air and g is the gravitational acceleration. The quantity ρ_0 is the reference value for dry air mass and $\varepsilon = 0.608$. The temperature fluctuations are given by $T'(x_j, t) = T(x_j, t) - \langle T(t) \rangle$ and the vapor mixing ratio fluctuations by $q'_v(x_j, t) = q_v(x_j, t) - \langle q_v(t) \rangle$ with $\langle \cdot \rangle$ being a volume average. The quantity c_p is the specific heat at constant pressure, L is the latent heat, κ the diffusivity of the temperature.

The additional term f_{LS} at right hand side of Eq. 2 keeps the flow in a statistically stationary state during the mixing process, i.e., throughout the simulation. This term is used is to model the driving of the entrainment process resulting from larger scales (LS) which go beyond the volume size considered here [4–6]. These equations are numerically solved on each grid points using pseudo-spectral method.

3 Data Set and HPC Systems

The computational domain of this simulation is a 3D cubic box having 4.096 m length in each direction. The grid size in all directions has been considered as 1 mm thus total number of grid points become $(4096)^3$. As described in mathematical model, total number of variable at each grid points are 5, namely, $\mathbf{u}, \mathbf{v}, \mathbf{w}, \mathbf{T}$ and $\mathbf{q_v}$. Each data file containing these variables has size of about 2.7 Terabytes (TB). The data was written parallelly in 'netcdf' format using 'pnetcdf' library [10]. In this file format each processor has an equal amount of data which is written to the file in parallel. The 'netcdf' format is a very common file format and is compatible with most visualization software. The main benefit of this file format is to analyze data using libraries such as NCL (NCAR Command Language) [7] which has been designed for visualization and scientific data analysis.

HPC system, named as "Pratyush", available at IITM has 4.0 PFlops computing capacity and is currently recognized as the fastest HPC system in India. It has total 3315 compute nodes with dual sockets, each having Intel Xeon Broadwell E52695 v4 18-core processors. Pratyush is a liquid cooled Cray XC40 supercomputer. This HPC system has total memory of 414 TB. All nodes are interconnected by the high speed, low latency Cray Aries NIC (Network Interface Controllers) with Dragonfly interconnect network topology which uses per packet adaptive routing. Furthermore, it has Lustre parallel file system [8]. This study presents optimization for the file system and benefits of using parallel I/O on Pratyush system which are detailed in next section.

4 Optimization Methodology

As stated before, this study attempts the optimization for parallel I/O as well as for computational time by using compiler flags. This section deals with first part of optimization which focuses on reducing the file processing time.

4.1 Lustre Optimization

Lustre is a type of parallel distributed file system, generally used for large-scale cluster computing. It is an open parallel file system which is used in HPC simulation environment [8]. The name Lustre is a portmanteau word derived from

Linux and cluster. Lustre file system software is available under the GNU General Public License (version 2 only) and provides high performance file systems for computer clusters ranging in size from small work group clusters to large-scale multi-site clusters. A Lustre file system is a high-performance shared file system for Linux clusters that is managed with Lustre software. It is highly scalable and can support several thousands of client nodes, multi-petabytes of storage, and hundreds of gigabytes per second of I/O throughput. Each Lustre file system is actually a set of many small file systems, which are referred to as Object Storage Targets (OSTs). The Lustre software presents the OSTs as a single unified file system. One of the main factors leading to the high performance of Lustre file systems is the ability to stripe data across multiple OSTs in a round-robin fashion. Basically, files can be split up into multiple chunks that will then be stored on different OSTs across the Lustre system.

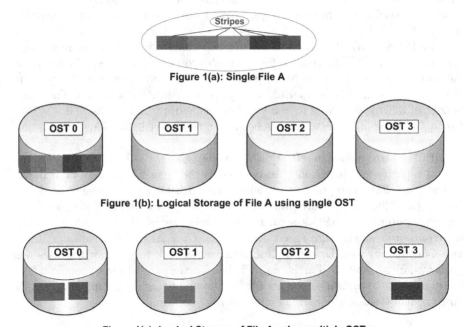

Figure 1(a): Single File A

Figure 1(b): Logical Storage of File A using single OST

Figure 1(c): Logical Storage of File A using multiple OSTs

Fig. 1. Panel (a) represents application view of a file stored in memory. The same file is stored using 1 OST which is depicted in panel (b) and using 4 OSTs in panel (c).

In the current case, the data files to be processed are huge, in particular, each file has size of 2.7 TB. The file processing time, that is time for reading and writing of file at once, is more than 1 h at 4096 cores. This processing time increases with increasing number of cores as shown in Fig. 2 depicting the writing times for different number of cores using 1 stripe.

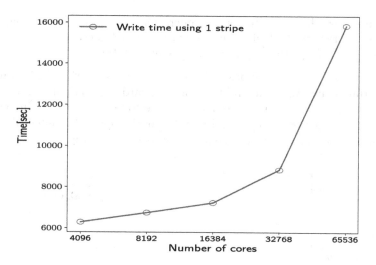

Fig. 2. Single file writing time using 1 stripe. The writing time increases as number of cores increases.

Eventually, it leads to increasing total simulation time enormously. The simulation for entrainment and mixing, used in this study, requires several such I/O operations, in particular, writing the data file at certain time steps. Therefore, to reduce the simulation time remains a challenge. The reduction in simulation time has been achieved by adopting different optimizations techniques described in following subsections.

4.2   Striping

Any file is just a linear sequence of bytes. The logical view of a file, divided into segments, is depicted in Fig. 1(a). Files on the Lustre file systems can be striped, which means they can be transparently divided into chunks that are written or read simultaneously across a set of OSTs within the file system. The chunks are distributed among the OSTs using a method that ensures load balancing. Pictorial representation of the striping of a file can be seen in Fig. 1(b). In the physical view, the five segments may be striped across four OSTs as shown in Fig. 1(b). On the Pratyush Cray XC40 system default stripe is set to 1.

Advantages: Striping offers two benefits;

(i) Increase in bandwidth utilization because multiple processes can simultaneously access the same file, and

(ii) The ability to store large files that would take more space than a single OST.

Disadvantages: However, striping is not without disadvantages, some of them are;

(i) Increased overhead due to network operations and server contention,
(ii) Increased risk of file damage due to hardware malfunction.
(iii) Load on OST by other application can cause bottleneck.

The Cray XC 40 systems has Aries interconnect network, which minimize the throttling issue. Also being robust machine, hardware malfunction while the file is writing is second to none. We have run the code using different number of striping increasing from 1 to 10 and found that the optimal number of stripes to reduce the file processing time should be 8 as shown in Fig. 3.

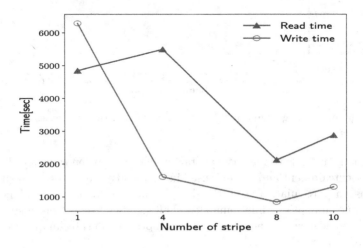

Fig. 3. Single file writing time using stripes from 1 to 10 when code is run with 4096 cores. The time reduces till 8 stripes thereafter starts increasing.

This figure shows that the writing time decreases till stripes 8 then it increases. In general, increasing number of OST should improve performance, i.e, reduces the file processing time. In ideal situation, no OST should be engaged by any other jobs. However, in this study all tests were carried out in real time situation when the system was also utilized by other jobs.

We have observed in some cases the file processing time decreases by utilizing 10 stripes in comparison to time taken with 8 stripes. Moreover, it was also observed that exploiting all the 10 OST, during real-time situations, was more likely to cause server contention. Hence, by considering all the available OSTs we have selected optimal number of OST as 8 with optimal stripe size 1 MB in this study. This optimal selection reduced the read/write time significantly.

Apart from striping technique; we have also attempted the IOBUF optimization which is detailed in next subsection.

4.3 IOBUF Optimizations

IOBUF is a library that intercepts standard I/O (stdio) and enables asynchronous caching and prefetching of sequential file access. Major advantage of using iobuf library is that no source code modification is required and it is easy to have control on I/O parameters using library options. By using these options, we were able to perform operations at higher speeds even when the checkpoint files were being written. However, it is to be noted that this library should not be used for;

(i) Hybrid programs that do I/O within a parallel region (not thread-safe).
(ii) Many processes accessing the same file in a coordinated fashion (MPI_File_write/read_all).

5   Results and Discussions

5.1   Parallel I/O Optimizations

The optimization experiments done here are mainly focused on high level file system and parallel I/O optimization. The computational domains for all experiments have $(4096)^3$ grid points.

First of all the striping techniques in OST have been attempted. By increasing the number of file stripes from 1 (the default value) to 8, the file writing time got reduced drastically. The file writing time for a single file, before optimization, was about 4 h using 65536 cores as evident from Fig. 2.

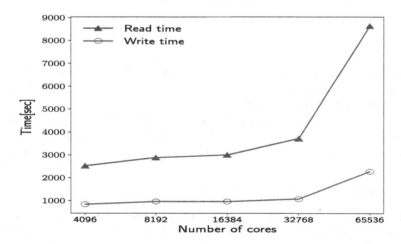

Fig. 4. Times (seconds) for reading and writing the file using striping technique. There is an increasing trend in file processing time when moving from small number cores to higher number cores.

Using the striping this time has come down as low as 38 min as shown in Table 1. The details of time reduction for other set of core numbers are also provided in this table. As can be seen from Table 1, the file I/O times have an increasing trend as we move from smaller number of cores to larger numbers.

Table 1. Average times (seconds) for a single file reading and writing after using file striping optimization (Striping + cray hugepages + no iobuf).

No. of cores	Reading time	Writing time
4K	2250	840
8K	2880	960
16K	3000	960
32K	3720	1080
65K	8640	2280

The increments in reading and writing times are 70% and 63% respectively as shown in Fig. 4. The striping optimization has significantly reduced total simulation time. Moreover, the file processing time after IOBUF optimization has reduced by about 14% as shown in Table 2.

Table 2. Total time comparison for 100 iterations after optimization (Striping + cray hugepages + iobuf). The main advantage of iobuf is reduction in writing time.

No. of cores	I/O operations	Total time (sec)
4K	With 2 reads, 2 writes	23120
4K with IOBUF	With 2 reads, 2 writes	19908

After these optimizations we have performed scaling of the code. Figure 5 represents the scaling of total time, without considering I/O time, for 500 iterations. This figure indicates that a linear scaling is observed till 16000 (actual number is 16384) cores thereafter, it starts degrading. Overall performance of the application showed good scaling. We have further attempted compiler level optimization, in particular, vectorization which is detailed in next sub section.

5.2   Vectorization

The Pratyush has Broadwell processors which supports the Advanced Vector Extensions 2 (AVX2). In this work, vectorization performances by flag 'AVX' and 'AVX2' have been compared. Application code was compiled using both the compiler flags. The 'xcore-AVX2', has features like doubling the number of peak floating-point operations and extension of Integer-vector instructions. Furthermore, the Broadwell processor has capability of enabling vector elements to be loaded from non-contiguous memory locations. The Flag AVX2 provided approximately 5% speedup when code was run on 4096 cores. The improved speed up may also be obtained due to availability of 2 FMAs (Fuses Multiply-Add) in Broadwell processor which further enhances computations. The comparison of simulation times using two vectorization flags (i.e., AVX and AVX2)

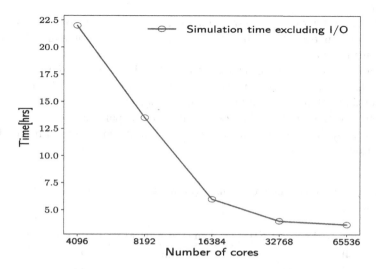

Fig. 5. Scaling of total time (in hours) excluding I/O time. The scaling is linear till 16K cores.

are presented in Table 3. To further reduce the total time we have used NUMA optimization which is theme of next subsection.

Table 3. Comparison of simulation times (for 50 iterations) using vectorization.

No. of cores	I/O operations	Total time (sec)
4K with AVX	With 1 reads, 1 writes	9005
4K with AVX2	With 1 reads, 1 writes	8555

5.3 NUMA Optimization

Each node in the Pratyush system has two Broadwell processors, that are having 64 GB of memory per socket thus, 128 GB in total for the whole node, which either processor can access. Each of these CPUs, with its corresponding memory, forms a NUMA node or NUMA-region. NUMA stands for Non Uniform Memory Access. It is generally much faster for a CPU to access its local NUMA node memory. Accessing the "remote" NUMA region will have higher latency and may slow down performance.

Moreover, each node in system has two CPU with 18 cores each thus, 36 cores aggregately. In this work, we have used 24 MPI cores out of the 36 which provided the best performance. This set of cores was chosen because of optimal utilization of RAM within a socket, i.e. to provide sufficient memory per thread for computation. Furthermore, a restriction of 12 cores per CPU was imposed.

Without this restriction, the system may consume all the 18 cores on one CPU and remaining 6 from the other one which may create imbalance for proper memory utilization.

The above memory management provided a significant performance boost. The simulation times excluding I/O time for 50 iterations with and without NUMA optimization are given in Table 4. The speedup has shown an increasing trends when more number of cores are utilized, in particular, for 32768 cores the performance has boosted up to 38%. This is a big contribution from NUMA optimization.

Table 4. Comparison of simulation times (for 50 iterations) with and without NUMA optimization.

Cores	Time (no NUMA)	Time (with NUMA)	Improvement
4K	21 h	19 h 44 min	6.0 %
8K	12 h 40 min	11 h 10 min	15.0 %
16K	5 h	4 h 10 min	16.8 %
32K	2 h 40 min	1 h 40 min	38.0 %

6   Conclusion and Outlook

The DNS code has been optimized using a high level file system and parallel I/O optimization. Four different types of optimization techniques were attempted. The optimization in parallel I/O, in particular the striping technique in Object Storage Targets (OSTs) of a file has drastically reduced the I/O time. Especially, the data file writing time has come down from 4 h to 38 min when running the simulation on 65536 cores. Employment of striping technique concludes that the DNS code having $(4096)^3$ grid points used in this work would give better performance using large number of cores (more than 16K). This conclusion is supported by scaling of code as shown in Fig. 5 which is linear up to 16K cores and time still goes down for more cores. Furthermore, file processing is required at specific time intervals which is not quite frequent providing the flexibility to run the code on higher number of cores.

Utilization of IOBUF library has further provided 14% reduction in file processing time. These two optimizations for parallel I/O provided a good speedup by reducing the I/O time. The compiler option, namely, AVX2 gave another 5% speedup in computational time. At last the NUMA optimization has added further time reduction of up to 38% (for 32768 cores) in the simulation time.

Further experimentation with hyper threading and multi-threading and use of advanced MPICH options can be attempted. One can also increase number of aggregators per OST which is expected to improve the performance as well as use of MPI I/O HINTS can be explored to exploit the benefits of data sieving.

Experiments in this study were conducted on 'scratch' file system having 10 OSTs. Prayush supercomputer has 52 OSTs in 'home' file system therefore, more experiments with additional OSTs can be attempted in future.

Acknowledgement. The HPC facilities at IITM Pune is fully funded by Ministry of Earth Science, Government of India.

References

1. Götzfried, P., Kumar, B., Shaw, R.A., Schumacher, J.: Droplet dynamics and fine-scale structure in a shearless turbulent mixing layer with phase changes. J. Fluid Mech. **814**, 452–483 (2017)
2. Heimsund, B., Espedal, S.M.: A parallel Eulerian-Lagrangian localised adjoint method. Adv. Water Resour. **23**, 950–955 (2005)
3. Herrman, M.: Parallel Eulerian interface tracking/Lagrangian point particle multi-scale coupling procedure. J. Comput. Phys. **229**, 745–759 (2020)
4. Kumar, B., Bera, S., Parabhakaran, T., Grabowski, W.W.: Cloud edge mixing: direct numerical simulation and observations in Indian monsoon cloud. J. Adv. Model. Earth Syst. **9**, 332–353 (2017). https://doi.org/10.1002/20016MS000731
5. Kumar, B., Schumacher, J., Shaw, R.A.: Cloud microphysical effects of turbulent mixing and entrainment. Theoret. Comput. Fluid Dyn. **27**, 361–376 (2013)
6. Kumar, B., Schumacher, J., Shaw, R.A.: Lagrangian mixing dynamics at the cloudy-clear air interface. J. Atmos. Sci. **71**(7), 2564–2580 (2014)
7. NCAR: NCL (NCAR Command Language). https://www.ncl.ucar.edu. Accessed 12 May 2018
8. Seagate Technology LLC United States: Lustre: the open source parallel file system. http://lustre.org. Accessed 12 May 2018
9. Stommel, H.: Entrainment of air into a cumulus cloud. J. Meteorol. **4**(91), 127–129 (1947)
10. Northwestern University, Argonne National Laboratory: Parallel netCDF: a parallel I-O library for netCDF file access. https://trac.mcs.anl.gov/projects/parallel-netcdf. Accessed 12 May 2018
11. Vaillancourt, P.A., Yau, M.K., Bartello, P., Grabowski, W.W.: Microscopic approach to cloud droplet growth by condensation. Part II: Turbulence, clustering and condensational growth. J. Atmos. Sci. **59**, 3421–3435 (2002)
12. Vaillancourt, P.A., Yau, M.K., Grabowski, W.W.: Microscopic approach to cloud droplet growth by condensation. Part I: Model description and results without turbulence. J. Atmos. Sci. **58**, 1945–1964 (2001)

Hybrid Parallelization of Particle in Cell Monte Carlo Collision (PIC-MCC) Algorithm for Simulation of Low Temperature Plasmas

Bhaskar Chaudhury[1]($\boxtimes$), Mihir Shah[1], Unnati Parekh[1], Hasnain Gandhi[1], Paramjeet Desai[1], Keval Shah[1], Anusha Phadnis[1], Miral Shah[1], Mainak Bandyopadhyay[2,3], and Arun Chakraborty[2]

[1] Group in Computational Science and HPC, DA-IICT, Gandhinagar 382007, India
bhaskar_chaudhury@daiict.ac.in
[2] ITER-India, Institute for Plasma Research (IPR), Gandhinagar 382428, India
[3] Homi Bhabha National Institute (HBNI), Anushakti Nagar, Mumbai 400094, India

Abstract. We illustrate the parallelization of PIC code, for kinetic simulation of Low Temperature Plasmas, on Intel Multicore (Xeon) and Manycore (Xeon Phi) architectures, and subsequently on a HPC cluster. The implementation of 2D-3v PIC-MCC algorithm described in the paper involves computational solution of Vlassov-Poisson equations, which provides the spatial and temporal evolution of charged-particle velocity distribution functions in plasmas under the effect of self-consistent electromagnetic fields and collisions. Stringent numerical constraints on total number of particles, number of grid points and simulation time-scale associated with PIC codes makes it computationally prohibitive on CPUs (serial code) in case of large problem sizes. We first describe a shared memory parallelization technique using OpenMP library and then propose a hybrid parallel scheme (OpenMP+MPI) consisting of a distributed memory system. OpenMP based PIC code has been executed on Xeon processor and Xeon-Phi co-processors (Knights Corner and Knights Landing) and we compare our results against a serial implementation on Intel core i5 processor. Finally, we compare the results of the hybrid parallel code with the OpenMP based parallel code. Hybrid strategy based on OpenMP and MPI, involving a three-level parallelization (instruction-level, thread-level over many cores and node-level across a cluster of Xeon processors), achieves a linear speedup on an HPC cluster with 4 nodes (total 64 cores). The results show that our particle decomposition based hybrid parallelization technique using private grids scale efficiently with increasing problem size and number of cores in the cluster.

1 Introduction

The Low Temperature Plasma (LTP) science and technology is a continuously growing interdisciplinary research area with broad range of applications [1].

© Springer Nature Singapore Pte Ltd. 2019
A. Majumdar and R. Arora (Eds.): SCEC 2018, CCIS 964, pp. 32–53, 2019.
https://doi.org/10.1007/978-981-13-7729-7_3

To aid the experimental investigations/developments in this area, several kinetic and fluid simulation models have been developed to study this complex medium consisting of electrons, ions, neutral atoms and molecules. Accurate simulation of plasmas using a kinetic model such as Particle-In-Cell (PIC) method plays an important role in the development of various plasma technologies [2]. PIC-MCC (Particle in Cell Monte Carlo Collision) method is a computationally expensive technique to investigate plasmas, and provides spatial and temporal evolution of the charged-particle velocity distribution functions under the effect of self-consistent electromagnetic (EM) fields and collisions [3,4]. In this method, we follow the trajectories of a representative number of charged particles in the phase space on a mesh free Lagrangian grid and take into account the collective interaction of the particles by solving Poisson's equation using an fixed point Euler grid [2–4]. The random sampling based Monte-Carlo Collisions (MCC) method is used to calculate the charged particle collisions with neutral atoms in PIC-MCC algorithm [2].

The dimensions of the phase-space, grid size, number of computational particles, time-step and total number of iterations required for the simulation [4] determines the computational cost of PIC codes. Compliance of several numerical constraints such as minimum grid spacing, minimum time step and minimum number of particles per cell (PPC) are often required for accurate simulation [2,4,5]. Typical run-times for PIC simulations ranges from several hours to months and requires advanced HPC facilities. The design and development of new high performance PIC codes for the exascale computing systems are topic of several recent investigations [6–8]. The paper by Hariri et al. describes the implementation of an efficient PIC simulation using OpenACC platform and reports about different parallelization strategies inspired by the newer technology in large scale computation [6]. Other major work which has benefited from the latest technological advancements includes development of PIC code by Derouillat et al. [7]. These works demonstrate the challenges in parallelization/optimization of PIC algorithm and why parallelization of PIC codes for emerging computing architectures is an important/challenging research problem.

Over the past several years, much effort has been put in to development of efficient parallel PIC codes for plasma simulation [9]. PIC code scaling for the 32 K nodes of Cray XT3 supercomputer using Fortran and MPI implementation have been reported in [10]. PIC-on-GPU [11], is a very well known open source implementation based on the Nvidia CUDA toolkit, which can scale to a GPU cluster if needed. Several strategies for parallelization of PIC codes on GPUs, for simulations of plasmas, have been reported recently. More details related to parallelization and optimization strategies of PIC codes reported in some of these works can be found in [4,6,8,12] and the references therein. The code developed by Decyk et al. [8] has different versions of the simulation specific to the architectures on which they are executed. The authors implement two new strategies for GPU, and suggested that highly efficient OpenMP implementation of the PIC code on core i7 shall work similarly on upcoming MIC architectures from Intel. In the recent article by Madduri et al. [13], the authors have presented an extensive comparison between various architectures for the computationally intensive charge deposition module. They have demonstrated the improvements arriving due to the newly developed methods of grid decomposition and synchronization against the existing strategies. The authors also extend this approach to the next generation of multi-core architectures.

The aim of this paper is to report about the development of an efficient double precision 2D-3v parallel PIC code optimized for the Intel multicore and manycore architectures, and subsequently a hybrid code (MPI+OpenMP) which runs on a CPU based cluster. Our work involves the development of a serial PIC-MCC code from scratch and validating it with published results from [14]. In this paper, firstly, we discuss the strategies used for efficient parallelization of the PIC code using openMP on Xeon processor and Xeon-Phi co-processors (Knights Corner and Knights Landing) and we compare our results against a serial implementation. Secondly, we describe the strategy for the hybrid implementation (using MPI+OpenMP) and we compare the performance results against the shared-memory based parallel code. Finally, we report and study the effect of simulation parameters such as grid size, number of particles and PPC on the run time of the hybrid code. The emergence of new hardware with more cores, better memory hierarchy and additional features such as vectorization is singularly not sufficient for solving the computational challenges of PIC simulations. The development of parallel algorithms needs to progress accordingly in order to achieve sustainable results. We focus our experimentation on the two generations of Xeon phi architectures, along with the Xeon processor for comparisons. However, because of high computational intensity and long simulation time, we need to develop a hybrid code which can be used to analyze larger problem sizes over longer time scales.

The paper is organized as follows: The computational model (PIC-MCC algorithm) is briefly described in Sect. 2. Section 3, gives an overview of the different architectures used in this work. Section 4 highlights the implementation details specific to our serial/parallel PIC-MCC code and a typical case study used for the validation of the code for modeling and simulation of a LTP experiment. Different parallelization strategies and optimization techniques are discussed in Sect. 5. The detailed performance analysis and important observations regarding performance results is given in Sect. 6, followed by conclusions in Sect. 7.

2   Computational Model

PIC is a self-consistent method wherein motion of charged particles is solved in the presence of self-consistent fields as well as externally applied EM field. When the current generated by plasma is low, the self induced magnetic field can be ignored and it is known as Electrostatic (ES) PIC method. The flowchart of self-consistent ES PIC-MCC method is shown in Fig. 1. The algorithm consists of following the trajectories of a representative number of charged particles in the phase space on a Lagrangian grid (mesh free) and describing the collective interaction of the particles by solving Poisson's equation using an Euler grid (fixed grid point) [3,4]. It involves splitting of the kinetic Valsov-Poisson equation (Eq. (1)) into two ordinary differential equations (Eqs. (2) and (3)).

$$\frac{\partial f}{\partial t} + v \cdot \frac{\partial f}{\partial x} + \frac{q}{m} \cdot \left(\boldsymbol{E} + \frac{\boldsymbol{v} \times \boldsymbol{B}}{c} \right) \cdot \frac{\partial f}{\partial v} = \left(\frac{\partial f}{\partial t} \right)_{colli} \tag{1}$$

$$\frac{d\boldsymbol{r}}{dt} = \boldsymbol{v} \tag{2}$$

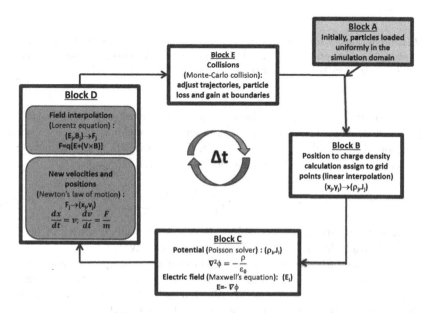

Fig. 1. Flowchart of the ES PIC-MCC algorithm [4]

$$\boldsymbol{F} = m\frac{d\boldsymbol{v}}{dt} = q \cdot \left(\boldsymbol{E} + \frac{\boldsymbol{v} \times \boldsymbol{B}}{c} \right) \tag{3}$$

The simulation domain is divided in spatial grids with grid size small enough (smaller than debye length) to resolve the variation in plasma parameters [3]. Initially, computational particles (representing electrons and ions) are uniformly loaded inside the simulation domain. Their initial positions and velocities are assigned randomly [15,16] (block **A** of Fig. 1). Maxwellian distribution is used for initialization of particle velocities.

Charge density is calculated on grid points from Lagrangian phase space information using linear interpolation weighing scheme (block **B** in Fig. 1) [4]. This is a computationally expensive part of the PIC-MCC method. A particle contributes its charge to the surrounding four points and this is accomplished by performing interpolation at every iteration for all particles as shown in Fig. 2. We

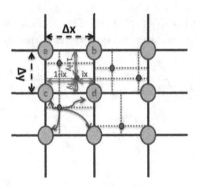

Fig. 2. Charge density assignment on grid points using linear interpolation. A, B, C and, D are grid points on the 2-D simulation grid. Green and black circles are particles inside different grid cells [4]. (Color figure online)

have used a linear interpolation scheme which is less noisy, and computationally cheaper compared to zeroth order and higher order schemes [3]. For example, contribution of a particle (shown in green in Fig. 2) towards charge density (ρ_A) on grid point A is calculated using the following equation,

$$\rho_A = q \left(\frac{ix \cdot iy}{\Delta x^2 \cdot \Delta y^2} \right) \tag{4}$$

where Δx and Δy are grid sizes, and ix, iy are fractional distances of particle from the cell origin in the x and y direction respectively.

Scalar potential from charge densities is calculated using Poisson's equation Eq. (5). An optimized, high performance and memory efficient PARDISO library is used to solve Poisson's equation [17]. Electric field E on grid points is derived by using finite difference form given in Eq. (6) (block **C** of Fig. 1).

$$\nabla^2 \phi = - \frac{\rho}{\epsilon_0} \tag{5}$$

$$\boldsymbol{E} = - \nabla \phi \tag{6}$$

New velocities and positions of particles are calculated using the newly computed field on Euler-grids. Euler grid to Lagrangian node transformation is accomplished by linear interpolation which is similar to the interpolation scheme described above for charge deposition. Force given by Eq. (3) is used to update equations of motion (Eqs. (2) and (3)) by using Boris method [18]. Mover (block **D** of Fig. 1) is also computationally intensive due to calculation of position and velocity of all the particles.

Finally, Monte-Carlo collisions (MCC, block **E** of Fig. 1) are applied to randomly selected particles using collision probability [16]. This method is used to select type of the collision and calculate the new particle velocities after collision [12].

The earliest works in the PIC code started with the development of 1-D code which was initially done to study the fluid dynamics calculations. The original code found various applications because of its efficient implementation in the massively parallel computers. This initial work laid the foundation of first electrostatic plasma model by the Bunneman's group at Stanford, and Birdsall and Bridges group at Berkeley [3]. Advancements in high performance and distributed computing have expanded the applicability of PIC method to broader spectrum of plasma science and technology [19].

3   Hardware and Programming Frameworks

Large scale highly parallel systems based on shared memory architectures are dominant computing platforms that give rise to many different parallel programming paradigms. **OpenMP** is a popular API for parallel programming on shared memory architecture. It uses a set of compiler directives (pragmas), library routines and environment variables to specify multi-threaded execution of the code. On distributed memory systems, **MPI** is widely used for writing message passing programs across nodes of a cluster. OpenMP based code can be also ported to emerging many-core architectures such as Intel Xeon-Phi [20]. Xeon Phi is a series of many-core processors. This vector processor has 256 bit wide SIMD registers and multiple cores. Its special vector processor helps in doing SIMD instructions faster. Depending on the version, it can do 4 or 8 double precision operations in the same time as a single operation on conventional processors. It supports four way multi-threading and has high bandwidth for on chip data access, which brings down latency to a great extent.

For small problem sizes, researchers generally use an OpenMP based code, however for bigger problem sizes and better accuracy we need hybrid codes. Thus, a combination of shared memory and message passing parallelization paradigms within the same application, often known as hybrid programming, is expected to provide more efficient parallelization strategy for clusters of shared memory nodes. The **hybrid OpenMP+MPI** programming refers to a programming style in which communication between nodes is handled by MPI processes and each MPI process has several OpenMP threads running inside to occupy the CPUs for computation.

Table 1 shows the four test benches which have been used in our work. The reference benchmark is a standard standalone CPU with 2 cores. But the hardware limitations of this CPU limits the grid sizes for which our simulation can be run. Thus, the serial code is parallelized using OpenMP and a high degree of thread level parallelism is achieved when it is run on the many-core architecture of the Intel Xeon Phi processors. When we develop the hybrid code, we run it on the 4 node cluster with shared memory multi-core processors, such that we get advantage of node-level parallelism as well.

Table 1. Specifications of the platforms used in our computational investigation. The compilation was done through the Intel Compiler 16.0.3 on all architectures. The compilation requires -fopenmp, -lpthread, -lm and -ldl flags. Other flags included are libiomp5.a, libmkl_blacs_openmpi_ilp64.a

	Reference	Bench 1	Bench 2	Bench 3	Bench 4
CPU	Intel i5-4210U Processor	Intel Xeon 2630, 2 sockets **(Xeon)**	Intel Xeon Phi 5110P Co-processor **(Phi 5)**	Intel Xeon Phi 7250 Processor **(Phi 7)**	4 node cluster: 2 Intel processor (E5-2640)/node
Frequency (GHz)	1.70	2.40	1.053	1.40	2.60
Cores	2	16	60	68	64
L2 size (MB)	0.25 (per core)	0.25 (per core)	30 (shared)	34 (shared)	-
L3 size (MB)	1.5 (per core)	20 (shared)	-	-	20 (shared)
Peak Memory Bandwidth (GB/s)	25.6 (2 channels)	59 (4 channels)	320 (16 channels)	115.2 (6 channels)	25.6 (2 channels)

4   Implementation Details and Code Validation

In this section, we present the details of the primary data structures used in our code. We also present the analysis of the code in terms of the arithmetic intensity in important subroutines and the execution time share of each subroutine followed by a case study for the validation of the code.

4.1   Data Structures

There are two essential groups of quantities associated with PIC simulations: Particle quantities and Grid quantities. As explained earlier, the particle to grid interpolations (for charge deposition) and the grid to particle interpolations (for moving the particles) are performed extensively. Hence, these quantities interact with each other very often.

In our $2D - 3v$ PIC code, for a specific computational particle representing many actual particles, particle quantities are the phase space information (position and velocity vectors) of that particle along with an identifier describing the species of that particle (electron or ion). These quantities are grouped into a structure which is named as *Particle* and to keep track of these quantities for every particle, an array of *Particle* structure is used as shown in Fig. 4(c).

Quantities such as charge density, potential, electric field, magnetic field have been discretized over the 2D grid. Since these quantities are recorded for every grid point, we have called them grid quantities. Each grid point has two components of electric field, one along X and the other along Y direction. Hence,

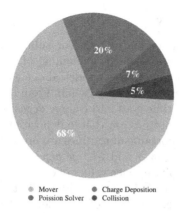

Mover ● Charge Deposition
● Poission Solver ● Collision

Fig. 3. The contribution of different modules/subroutines towards the total run-time of the serial code for a typical simulation (moderate problem size) [4]. Grid size of 1024×1024 with 20 PPC density simulation. Executed on a single core of Intel Xeon E5-2630 v3 with 64 GB of DDR3 RAM. *Mover* and *Charge Deposition* prevail the overall execution time.

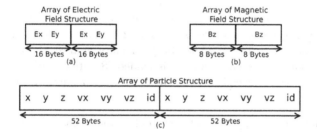

Fig. 4. Visualization of particle and grid data structure. (a) Electric field components are stored as an array of structure. (b) Magnetic field has only one component, so it is stored in an array of double data type. (c) Every particle has their own phase space information stored in a Particle structure. Hence, information of all particles is stored as an array of structures [4].

electric field information is stored in a structure for a particular grid point and an array of these structures is used to maintain the information of electric field for the whole grid. The magnetic field for our simulation purpose has been kept varying only in the Z direction. Hence, only the array of values is needed to keep track of magnetic field over all grid points. Same is the case for charge density and electric potential. All the quantities (particle and grid) are stored as double precision floating point values during the simulation. An important point to note here is that even though the grid quantities are over the grid points of a 2D grid, but when storing it as an array, we have used just a 1D array rather than using the 2D array (array of arrays) [4].

4.2   Arithmetic Intensity

[1]Arithmetic intensity of a section of code (or subroutine) is the ratio of the number of computations performed to the number of bytes transferred from/to memory in that code section and gives an idea about whether the section (module or subroutine) is compute or memory bound. From the Fig. 3, we can see that the most of the simulation time goes into *Charge deposition* and *Mover* module. Hence, the important subroutines are charge deposition and mover. The arithmetic intensity of these important subroutines are presented in Table 2 and from that we can see that both *Mover* and *Charge deposition* are memory bound.

Mover needs to load 6 phase space values of 8 bytes each and another 4 bytes are needed to identify the type of particle – id attribute of Particle structure as shown in Fig. 4(c). Based on the type of particle, we have to fetch the charge to mass ratio for that particle which requires 8 bytes to be fetched. 12 values corresponding to E_x, E_y and B_z on four cell corners (8 bytes each) are read to interpolate the fields on to the particles as shown in Fig. 2. Finally, all the 6 phase space values are updated (8 bytes each). The rest of the data is for keeping track of the different particle types and their start index in the particle data structure.

In *Charge Deposition*, x and y coordinates of the particle along with an identifier for the type of particle is loaded (20 bytes total). Weighing factor (8 bytes) is required to balance the charge density against the actual number of particles. Finally, the charge density is loaded (8 bytes each) and updated (8 bytes each) on all the four cell corners. Rest of the data is used for book keeping.

Table 2. Arithmetic intensity (ratio of number of computations to the number of bytes transferred from/to memory) [4].

	Mover	CD
Double-precision operations (FLOP)	91	19
Double-precision Read/Write (Byte)	204	92
Arithmetic intensity (FLOP/Byte)	0.446	0.206

4.3   Code Validation and Comparison of Simulations with Experiment

One of the important application of PIC-MCC method is in investigation of Low Temperature Plasmas involving transport of charged particles across magnetic field. The physics of plasma transport across strong magnetic field is a complex phenomenon and present in many applications including fusion reactors, thruster and also in negative ion sources. We have used this standard problem for validating our PIC-MCC code [12,14] and particularly to simulate the collisional transport across magnetic filters under conditions similar to real ROBIN

---

[1] The text in this particular subsection has been adopted from [4].

negative ion source experiment. ROBIN (Rf operated Beam source in India for Negative ion research) has been setup at IPR, Gandhinagar to understand and investigate the different issues related to production, transport and extraction of negative hydrogen ions in negative ion sources for fusion applications [21]. The source consists of a driver, an expansion chamber, a transverse magnetic filter field (TMF) and extraction grids as shown in Fig. 5. Simulation domain, considered for this study, takes into account 2-D displacements of particles in X-Y plane with 3 velocity components under the influence of an externally applied magnetic field (B_z) perpendicular to the simulation domain (in z direction with Gaussian shape variation in x direction [14]). The spatial grid size in the computational domain is small enough to resolve the important physical length scales such as electron Debye length. Temporal time steps are chosen such that it can resolve important time scales of the system and is generally given by Courant-Friedrichs-Lewy (CFL) condition $\Delta t \leq \frac{0.2}{\omega_p}$. Using this code (number of grid points $= 800 \times 154$, grid size $= 6.5\text{E}-4\,\text{m}$, time step $= 1.2\,\text{E}-10\,\text{s}$, initial number of electrons and ions $= 2.5$ million each), we have investigated different plasma characteristics such as plasma potential, electron temperature, electron and ion density profiles, electric field, current etc. (as shown in Fig. 5) in the case of a Gaussian shaped magnetic filter, as a case. Simulation results show similar qualitative and quantitative behaviors as observed during the first phase of ROBIN experiments.

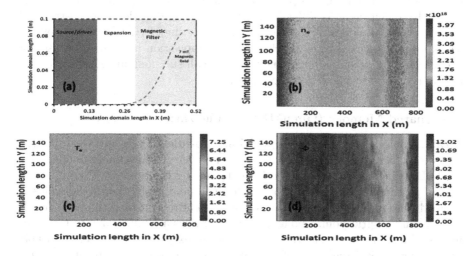

Fig. 5. (a) Schematic of the computational domain. Sub-figures (b, c, d) shows the profile of the electron density, electron temperature and potential at $72\,\mu\text{s}$ of physical time.

5   Parallelization Strategy

The parallelization of PIC code serves as a major research problem in the area of High Performance Computing. The earliest works on parallelizing the PIC codes were designed for distributed memory systems. The nodes simply communicate using message passing, no shared memory is available to take advantage of thread level parallelism [22]. This approach does not scale for larger problem sizes [8]. With the advancements of shared memory parallelism, researchers tried to implement PIC code using OpenMP library. This method also suffers from similar problem of scalability [7].

Newer methods for parallelizing PIC codes are based on distributed systems with shared memory parallelization in each node. This system uses the hybrid MPI+OpenMP programming technique which is the focus of this paper. There are two ways in which hybrid parallelization is achieved. These are particle and grid based decomposition.

The particle-based decomposition is widely used because of its easy implementation and near perfect load balance [7]. The hybrid programming paradigm used in this paper implements OpenMP based thread level shared memory parallelization inside MPI based node level processes, i.e., each MPI node has a fixed number of OpenMP threads and which communicate among MPI processes outside the parallel region.

The grid-based decomposition is based on sharing a part of grid among different nodes rather than the particles. This method suffers from the problem of load balancing as it is difficult to ensure that the particles are distributed equally among all nodes. A similar method consisting of very fine-grain domain decomposition referred to as patch-based decomposition has also been used in recent works [7], where patches denote very small sub domains. This method is an extension of grid-based decomposition.

5.1   Shared Memory (OpenMP) Parallelization Strategy

Parallelization of Charge Deposition Module. There are two different strategies which can be used to parallelize the *Charge Deposition* module.

(1) Dividing the rows of the grid equally among the threads. The interpolations of all the particles lying in one region will be done by the thread which is assigned that region. If each thread shares the entire grid then the two threads having common grid points along the common rows are vulnerable to race conditions. Therefore we must give each thread an exclusive portion of the whole grid. To get a consistent view of grid quantities, we need to aggregate the grid quantities shared between two threads at the boundary. Due to the continuous movement of the particles in the computational domain, it is very likely that there are unequal number of particles across the different areas of the grid and hence unequal number of particles per thread which may lead to **uneven load balancing**. Moreover, each thread must exactly know the particles that are lying in the region assigned to it along with the location of those particles in the array of particles. To do this efficiently, the particles lying in one region have to be

grouped together in the array of particles. The start and end index of that group has to be calculated. This grouping has to be done after every iteration since the particles will be moving continuously throughout the simulation. Doing this at every iteration introduces extra overhead and complexity.

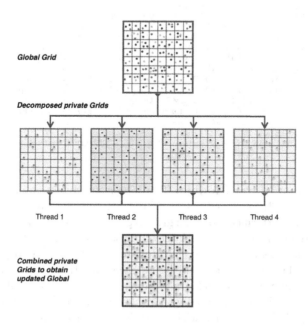

Global Grid

Decomposed private Grids

Thread 1   Thread 2   Thread 3   Thread 4

Combined private
Grids to obtain
updated Global

Fig. 6. Parallelization strategy for charge deposition module.

(2) Dividing equal number of particles among the threads. This strategy is motivated by the Principle of Superposition. Since the interpolations in this module applies as particle-to-grid, the race conditions may arise when two different particles handled by two different threads try to update the grid quantities pertaining to the same grid point simultaneously. In order to avoid race conditions we shall assign each thread a private copy of the global grid as portrayed in Fig. 6. This ensures that each thread works independently on its share of particles without any critical region or requirement for locks. Once the threads have done their share of calculating grid quantities on their own private grids, we aggregate all the private grids to get back the global grid. This strategy involves the overhead of generating private grids for each thread. Synchronization is straightforward.

Out of these two strategies, the second approach would result in efficient load balancing among all the threads as compared to the first one. Also, if we increase the problem size, the latter strategy is scalable since the time taken to synchronize the whole grid is negligible compared to the time taken to perform particle to grid interpolations.

We have used the second strategy in our implementation and the following is the **pseudo-code for parallel execution of charge deposition module.**

```
1  void chargeDeposition()
2      GridQty *private_grid_qty = malloc(no_of_threads * GRID_DIMENSIONS);
3      /* Parallelization over particles using private grids */
4      #pragma omp parallel for
5      for(i = 0; i < total_particles; i++)
6          int id = omp_get_thread_num();
7          /* Position of neighboring grid points */
8          double x1, y1, x2, y2, x3, y3, x4, y4;
9          /* Calculate the position of neighboring grid points
10         based on the position information from particle_array[i] */
11         double update1, update2, update3, update4; /* Updates */
12         /* Calculate the value of updates */
13         /* Update the private grid quantity's value at nearby grid points */
14         private_grid_qty[id * GRID_DIMENSIONS + x1 * Nx + y1] += update1;
15         private_grid_qty[id * GRID_DIMENSIONS + x2 * Nx + y2] += update2;
16         private_grid_qty[id * GRID_DIMENSIONS + x3 * Nx + y3] += update3;
17         private_grid_qty[id * GRID_DIMENSIONS + x4 * Nx + y4] += update4;
18     /* Combine the private grids to form the updated global (Synchronization) */
19     for(i = 0; i < no_of_threads; i++)
20         for(j = 0; j < Nx * Ny; j++)
21             global_grid[j] = private_grid_qty[i * GRID_DIMENSIONS + j];
```

Parallelization of Mover Module. The *Mover* subroutine can be parallelized by dividing the particles equally among the threads. In this subroutine, the interpolations are performed from the grid to particle. Since particles are divided among the threads, a particular particle's phase space information is updated only once by one thread and to do that update, the thread has to just read the grid quantities. Therefore, there will be no race conditions while updating the phase space information of particles in parallel. Hence, this is an embarrassingly-parallel challenge. Moreover, dividing particles equally among the threads will lead to efficient load balancing with a straightforward implementation using static scheduling.

```
1  void mover()
2      /* Parallelization over particles using private grids */
3      #pragma omp parallel for
4      for(i = 0; i < total_particles; i++)
5          double updateX, updateY; /* Updates in position */
6          double updateVx, updateVy, updateVz; /* Updates in velocities */
7          /* Calculate the value of updates based on the value of
8          grid quantities at neighboring grid points */
9          /* Update the phase space information at particle_array[i] */
10         particles_array[i].x += updateX; particles_array[i].y += updateY;
11         particles_array[i].vx += updateVx; particles_array[i].vy += updateVy;
12         particles_array[i].vz += updateVz;
```

Sorting. It has been well established that sorting significantly increases simulation speeds of PIC and eliminates cache thrashing [23]. Cache thrashing occurs while interpolation of quantities from the grid to the particles and particles to grid. If the particle array is sorted based on their positions in the grid, the grid quantities are no more accessed randomly and hence this strategy successfully achieves cache re-usability.

We performed experiments on different architectures to inspect when sorting leads to increase in speedup. The results can be seen in Fig. 7(a). For processors with smaller cache sizes, the grid data structures used in the simulation cannot fit in the cache completely and thus, sorting helps in improving their performance. But for systems with very large cache size like in the Intel Xeon Phi co-processors and those commonly used today, the grid data structures are able to easily fit in the cache. Thus, sorting adds unnecessary overhead in this case and leads to lower speed up than expected. Therefore, we are not sorting the particles before the charge deposition module.

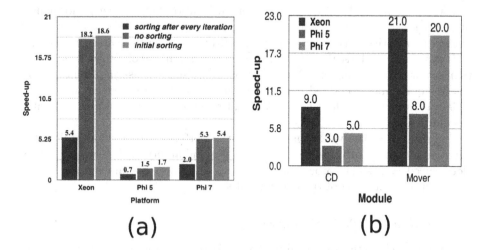

(a)   **(b)**

Fig. 7. (a) Strategy-wise maximum speed-up of optimized parallel execution on 3 different architectures relative to a non-sorted serial execution on the Intel i5 processor. (b) Module-wise maximum speed-up on selected architectures (different number of threads on different architectures). This value is calculated relative to a serial execution on an Intel i5 based machine.

Table 3. Cache hit rate comparison (perf analysis). This observation is in accordance with the fact that Phi-7 architecture has a significantly larger cache than the Xeon architecture (Table 1).

	Serial	Parallel
Xeon	88.24	76.22
Phi 7	95.66	86.88

The numerical results in Fig. 7(b) and the supporting figures have been obtained through guidelines laid down by Hoefller [24]. For analyzing the behavior of strategies on varying architectures, we chose a base architecture (Intel i5) to act as a common reference (Table 1).

There is an extensive variation in the sequential code execution time of the architectures that we have considered for analysis. The values range from 140 s on Intel Xeon E5-2630 (**Xeon**), 386 s on Intel i5, 971 s on Intel Xeon Phi 7250 (**Phi 7**) and 3892 s on Intel Xeon Phi 5110p (**Phi 5**). The simulation corresponds to a physical time of 18 ns on a square grid of 128-128 partitions with a density of 20 particles per cell. Due to this significant difference in the serial processing power; theoretically, a perfectly parallel code executed on Xeon Phi 5110p with 28 cores will perform at par with the same serial version executed on E5-2630.

Xeon Phi has a more primitive prefetching, slower clock frequency, in-order processing, a smaller pipeline, one instruction per two cycles etc. Therefore, the key to best performance is doing the best optimization in all the three aspects: vectorization, parallelization, and memory utilization. The under-performance of our execution can be explained through the very low vectorization potential of the PIC algorithm as supported by the arithmetic intensity values in Table 2. This explains why the scalar code running on a single thread of Xeon Phi is slower than scalar code running on a Xeon. This is a problem because the scalar unit of Phi 5 is quite under-powered, both for itself and relative to modern processors. This was improved in the Phi 7 but it still remains slower in comparison with the multi-core Xeon.

Inferring from the values in Fig. 7(b), the performance of the overall optimization is significantly specific to the features and ability of the hardware. The clock speed of a single processor, cache size and cores are among the major contributors in shaping of the above results.

5.2 Hybrid Parallelization Strategy

For system architectures enabled for hybrid parallelization, we can make use of multiple nodes connected to each other via the network. We use the MPI library to enable communication between the nodes (*Node-level parallelism*). Each node has a specific number of cores and each core, in turn, is capable of launching hardware threads (*Thread level parallelism*).

Let us revisit the parallelization strategies discussed in Sect. 5.1 to extend them to the hybrid implementation. The parallelization of the *Charge Deposition* module has been achieved using OpenMP. The particles are equally divided among the OpenMP threads and each thread has its own private copy of the grid quantities to avoid race conditions when performing particle to grid interpolation. Once all the OpenMP threads have updated their private copies of the grid quantities, these private copies are aggregated to get the updated global grid. This ensures that the grid quantities are consistent before and after the *Mover* module is executed. For the parallelization of the *Mover* module, the particles are equally divided among the OpenMP threads, as a solution to an embarrassingly parallel sub-problem.

The hybrid parallelization strategy naturally builds from the strategy used for thread level parallelization which is summarized above. At the beginning of the simulation, the particles are equally divided among the nodes as shown in the Level 1 parallelization of Fig. 8. Each node is responsible for executing the *Charge deposition* and *Mover* module for the set of particles that are assigned/private to that node. Since the particles are divided among nodes, each node is required to have its own private copy of the grid in order to avoid race conditions with the other nodes during the *Charge deposition* subroutine. After the execution of the

Charge deposition module, the private copies of each node must be aggregated to get consistent view of grid quantities on global level.

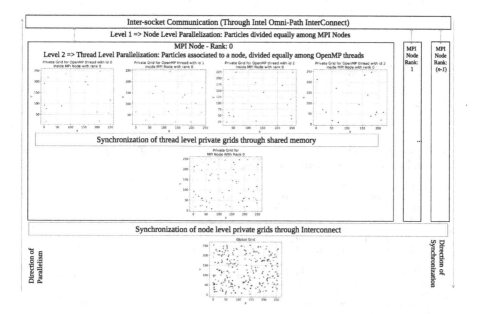

Fig. 8. Visualization of the hybrid parallelization strategy. Level 1 (node-level parallelization): particle distribution per node and the aggregation of private grids of all nodes and Level 2 (thread level parallelization inside a node): further distribution of particles of a node per thread and the synchronization of private grids per thread to get a consistent private grid per node

Since each node has multiple cores, it shall execute the thread level parallelization strategy explained in Sect. 5.1 for the *Charge Deposition* module for the particles assigned to that node to get the updated node-level grid quantities. Once each node has its own private copy of grid quantities updated, each node takes part in the global node-level aggregation of the grid quantities through its own private grid quantities.

For this global aggregation, each node must use the network and communicate to every other node its private copy of grid quantities. Post this communication between nodes, the grid quantities are consistent among all the private node grids. Since, this aggregation takes place over the network, it is expensive communication. It is important to reduce this cost, by optimizing it using the `MPI_Allreduce` function provided by MPI library.

5.3   Pseudo-code of Hybrid Parallelization Strategy

At the beginning of the PIC simulation, the data about initial conditions of the simulation is read from a file. That file contains information about the total

number of computational particles in the simulation. Each MPI node reads the
file and is allotted the number of particles that it is supposed to handle as follows:

```
1  int particles_for_this_node = total_particles / MPI_WORLD_SIZE
2  if (mpi_world_rank == MPI_WORLD_SIZE − 1):
3      particles_for_this_node += (total_particles % MPI_WORLD_SIZE)
4  /* Memory allocations for the Particle array based on
5  the total number of particles assigned to this node */
6  Particle *particle_array = malloc(particles_for_this_node)
7  /* Memory allocations for private grids */
8  GridQty1 *private_grid_qty_1 = malloc(GRID_DIMENSIONS)
9  GridQty2 *private_grid_qty_2 = malloc(GRID_DIMENSIONS)
10 ...
11 GridQtyN *private_grid_qty_n = malloc(GRID_DIMENSIONS)
12 /* Other initializations */
```

Once these initialization are complete, each node enters the simulation loop.
The pseudo-code for the simulation loop is as follows:

```
1  while (simulation_not_over):
2      /* Execution of charge deposition module,
3      using the thread level parallelization */
4      chargeDeposition();
5      /* Global synchronization of private node−level copies of grid quantities */
6      MPI_Allreduce(private_grid_qty_1, ...)
7      MPI_Allreduce(private_grid_qty_2, ...)
8      ...
9      MPI_Allreduce(private_grid_qty_n, ...)
10     /* After the call to Allreduce, each node has
11     consistent view of grid quantities */
12     /* Execution of mover module using the thread level parallelization */
13     mover(grid_qty)
14     /* Other modules of the PIC simulation */
```

6   Results

As the grid size increases, while keeping the Particle Per Cell (PPC) value constant, then the number of particles also increases. Therefore, the memory consumption also increases for both grid and particle data structures. In the Table 4,
we have reported the memory consumption of grid data structures used to store
electric and magnetic fields, and the memory consumption of the particle data
structure. Similar amount of memory is also used for other grid based data structures such as electron number density, ion number density, charge density, energy
and potential. The memory taken by one element of the respective data structure is reported in the Sect. 4.1. It is evident from the first column of the Table 4
that the memory needed to store the array of particles increases drastically as
we increase the grid size.

The biggest advantage of our hybrid parallelization strategy is in terms of
memory consumption. Since the particles are divided equally among the nodes,
even if we increase the grid size, the memory used to store all the particles
would increase but it would be less per node when compared to the OpenMP
parallelization strategy in which the array of particles would have been stored
in just one node. This analysis is shown in the Table 4.

Table 4. Memory consumed in MBs by the particle and grid data structures - Electric Field (EF) and Magnetic Field (MF) per each MPI node - in the parallelization achieved using OpenMP and the hybrid parallelization strategy for different problem size and fixed particle per cell(PPC) value of 80.

Grid size	OpenMP with 4 cores			Hybrid with 4 nodes, 4 core each			Hybrid with 8 nodes, 4 core each		
	Particle array size (MB)	EF array size (MB)	MF array size (MB)	Particle array size (MB)	EF array size (MB)	MF array size (MB)	Particle array size (MB)	EF array size (MB)	MF array size (MB)
512×512	1040	4	2	260	4	2	130	4	2
1024×1024	4160	16	4	1060	16	4	520	16	4
2048×2048	16640	64	16	4160	64	16	2080	64	16

Table 5. Comparison of the execution time (in seconds) taken by the OpenMP code run on 4 cores (Bench 1 of Table 1) and the Hybrid code run on different number of nodes each having some number of cores (Bench 4 of Table 1, using all 4 nodes) for 100 iterations of the simulation with different grid sizes and particle per cell(PPC) values.

Grid size	Run time (sec) for 40 PPC			Run time (sec) for 80 PPC		
	OpenMP 1 node, 4 cores per node	Hybrid 4 nodes, 4 cores per node	Hybrid 8 nodes, 4 cores per node	OpenMP 1 node, 4 cores per node	Hybrid 4 nodes, 4 cores per node	Hybrid 8 nodes, 4 cores per node
512×512	64.26	26.48	18.55	115.97	43.16	25.74
1024×1024	457.36	146.35	92.96	972.47	254.44	157.82
2048×2048	2380.07	709.87	427.65	4770.77	1592.25	681.88

Table 6. Comparison of the speedup for hybrid system with different number of MPI nodes for 100 iterations of the simulation with different grid sizes and particle per cell(PPC) values. Here, Speedup = execution time of OpenMP based code on a multi-core processor with 4 cores (Bench 1)/execution time of corresponding hybrid system (Bench 4)

Grid size	Speedup for 40 PPC		Speedup for 80 PPC	
	Hybrid 4 nodes, 4 cores per node	Hybrid 8 nodes, 4 cores per node	Hybrid 4 nodes, 4 cores per node	Hybrid 8 nodes, 4 cores per node
512×512	2.42	3.46	2.69	4.51
1024×1024	3.13	4.92	3.82	6.16
2048×2048	3.35	5.57	3.00	7.00

As we can see from the Tables 5 and 6, if we keep the number of nodes fixed then the speedup increases when we increase the problem size, i.e., increasing the grid size and/or increasing the particle per cell(PPC). Also, for large problem size, increasing the number of cores/node leads to increase in the speedup indicating the code scales well for architectures with many nodes or cores/node. One reason for this is that as we increase the problem size, the aggregation of the node-level private copy of grid quantities through MPI_Allreduce takes negligible time compared to the time taken in performing extensive interpolations for large number of particles per node.

Table 7. Comparison of the execution time (in seconds) of the Mover module for the hybrid code with different number of cores and different problem size and fixed PPC value of 80.

Grid size	Time (sec) – Mover		
	OpenMP 1 node, 4 cores per node	Hybrid 4 nodes, 4 cores per node	Hybrid 8 nodes, 4 cores per node
512×512	71.42	17.24	8.66
1024×1024	540.023	113.97	53.90
2048×2048	2768.83	622.98	295.51

Table 8. Speedup of the Mover module for the hybrid code with different number of cores and different problem size and fixed PPC value of 80. Here, Speedup = execution time of OpenMP based code on a multi-core processor with 4 cores (Bench 1)/execution time of corresponding hybrid system (Bench 4)

Grid size	Speedup – Mover	
	Hybrid 16 cores	Hybrid 32 cores
512×512	4.14	8.24
1024×1024	4.73	10.02
2048×2048	4.44	9.37

As shown in the Fig. 3, the *Poisson Solver* and *Collision* modules take negligible fraction of time out of the whole computation time. Therefore, we have only reported the results for the *Mover* module in Tables 7 and 8. As can be seen from the Table 8, for large problem sizes, the *Mover* module give superlinear speedup (marginally), suggesting that they are able to efficiently use the (combined) cache compared to the OpenMP implementation.

Also, from the results of Table 8 one can see that the speedup is maximum when the grid size is 1024×1024 and the speedup for 2048×2048 is lesser than that when grid size is 1024×1024. One plausible explanation for this is that as we increase the grid size, after a point it is not possible to accommodate the entire Electric and Magnetic field's grid in the cache, as can be observed from the Table 4. For the specific case of 1024×1024 grid size, the grids barely fit in the cache for the hybrid code as well as OpenMP code but the cache utilization for this specific grid size is much more significant for hybrid code than its OpenMP counterpart.

7   Conclusion

We have proposed and investigated in detail an optimized shared memory parallelization strategy of the PIC-MCC algorithm for plasma simulation on Intel Xeon-Phi (many-core) and Xeon (multi-core) architectures as well as an efficient hybrid (OpenMP+MPI) implementation which can be easily implemented on a HPC cluster consisting of nodes with multi-core processors. In order to take advantage of recent advancements in architectures supporting hybrid parallelization, our hybrid parallelization strategy is a natural extension of the shared memory parallelization strategy which requires minimal changes in the code. Our numerical experiments with different problem sizes reveal that for large problem sizes it becomes increasingly difficult to use just the shared memory parallelization strategy because of the limited access to shared primary memory. But the hybrid parallelization strategy makes such large scale simulations possible as it makes use of a large number of nodes such that the particles fit in the primary memory of their respective nodes. Also, unlike other previous strategies based on grid decomposition, our particle decomposition strategy scales very efficiently with increasing number of nodes. We also observe that unlike Xeon multi-core architecture, observed speedup is below expectation in case of Xeon-Phi MIC processors due to lack of scope of vectorization of PIC algorithm and other limiting factors pertaining to serial executions on Xeon-Phi. Efficient hybrid PIC codes opens up many possibilities for research in the area of Low Temperature Plasmas which require computationally intensive PIC-MCC simulations.

Acknowledgement. The work has been carried out using the HPC facilities at DA-IICT and hardware received under BRNS-PFRC project. We would also like to acknowledge the help received from Colfax's remote access program. We thank Siddarth Kamaria, Harshil Shah and Riddhesh Markandeya for their contribution towards the serial code development. Miral Shah thanks Department of Atomic Energy, Govt. of India for junior research fellowship (JRF) received under BRNS-PFRC project (No. 39/27/2015-BRNS/34081).

References

1. Adamovich, I., et al.: The 2017 plasma roadmap: low temperature plasma science and technology. J. Phys. D: Appl. Phys. **50**(32), 323001 (2017)
2. Birdsall, C.K., Langdon, A.B.: Plasma Physics via Computer Simulations. CRC Press, Boca Raton (1991)
3. Birdsall, C.K., Fellow, L.: Particle-in-cell charged-particle simulations, plus Monte Carlo collision with neutral atom, PIC-MCC. IEEE Trans. Plasma Sci. **19**(2), 65–85 (1991)
4. Shah, H., Kamaria, S., Markandeya, R., Shah, M., Chaudhury, B.: A novel implementation of 2D3V particle-in-cell (PIC) algorithm for Kepler GPU architecture. In: IEEE 24th International Conference on High Performance Computing (HiPC), pp. 378–387 (2017)
5. Verboncoeur, J.P.: Particle simulation of plasmas: review and advances. Plasma Phys. Control. Fusion **47**(5A), A231–A260 (2005)
6. Hariri, F., et al.: A portable platform for accelerated PIC codes and its application to GPUs using OpenACC. Comput. Phys. Commun. **207**, 69–82 (2016)
7. Derouillat, J., et al.: SMILEI: a collaborative, open-source, multi-purpose particle-in-cell code for plasma simulation. Comput. Phys. Commun. **222**, 351–373 (2018)
8. Decyk, V.K., Singh, T.V.: Particle-in-cell algorithms for emerging computer architectures. Comput. Phys. Commun. **185**(3), 708–719 (2014)
9. Carmona, E.A., Chandler, L.J.: On parallel PIC versatility and the structure of parallel PIC approaches. Concurr. Comput.: Pract. Exp. **9**, 1377–1405 (1997)
10. Adams, M.F., Ethier, S., Wichmann, N.: Performance of particle in cell methods on highly concurrent computational architectures. J. Phys.: Conf. Ser. **78**, 012001 (2007)
11. Burau, H., et al.: PIConGPU: a fully relativistic particle-in-cell code for a GPU cluster. IEEE Trans. Plasma Sci. **38**(10), 2831–2839 (2010)
12. Claustre, J., Chaudhury, B., Fubiani, G., Paulin, M., Boeuf, J.P.: Particle-in-cell monte carlo collision model on GPU-application to a low-temperature magnetized plasma. IEEE Trans. Plasma Sci. **41**(2), 391–399 (2013)
13. Madduri, K., Su, J., Williams, S., Oliker, L., Ethier, S., Yelick, K.: Optimization of parallel particle-to-grid interpolation on leading multicore platforms. IEEE Trans. Parallel Distrib. Syst. **23**(10), 1915–1922 (2012)
14. Boeuf, J.P., Chaudhury, B., Garrigues, L.: Physics of a magnetic filter for negative ion sources. I. Collisional transport across the filter in an ideal, 1D filter. Phys. Plasmas **19**(11), 113509 (2012)
15. Fehske, H., Schneider, R., Weibe, A.: Computational Many-Particle Physics. Lecture Notes in Physics, vol. 739. Springer, Heidelberg (2008). https://doi.org/10.1007/978-3-540-74686-7
16. Tskhakaya, D., Matyash, K., Schneider, R., Taccogna, F.: The particle-in-cell method. Contrib. Plasma Phys. **47**(8–9), 563–594 (2007)
17. Schenk, O., Gartner, K.: Solving unsymmetric sparse systems of linear equations with PARDISO. Futur. Gener. Comput. Syst. **20**(3), 475–487 (2004)
18. Boris, J.P.: Relativistic plasma simulation-optimization. In: 4th Conference on Numerical Simulation of Plasma, no. November 1970, p. 3 (1970)
19. Lapenta, G.: Particle-based simulation of plasmas. In: Plasma Modeling. IOP Publishing, Bristol (2016). https://doi.org/10.1088/978-0-7503-1200-4ch4. Chap. 4
20. Sodani, A., et al.: Knights landing: second-generation Intel Xeon Phi product. IEEE Micro **36**(2), 34–46 (2016)

21. Bansal, G., et al.: Negative ion beam extraction in ROBIN. Fusion Eng. Des. **88**, 778–782 (2013)
22. Rabenseifner, R.: Hybrid parallel programming on HPC platforms. In: Fifth European Workshop on OpenMP, EWOMP 2003, Aachen, Germany, 22–26 September 2003 (2003)
23. Bowers, K.: Accelerating a particle-in-cell simulation using a hybrid counting sort. J. Comput. Phys. **173**, 393–411 (2001)
24. Hoefler, T., Belli, R.: Scientific benchmarking of parallel computing systems: twelve ways to tell the masses when reporting performance results. In: Proceedings of the International Conference for High Performance Computing, Networking, Storage and Analysis, p. 73 (2015)

A Review of Dimensionality Reduction in High-Dimensional Data Using Multi-core and Many-core Architecture

Siddheshwar V. Patil$^{(\boxtimes)}$ and Dinesh B. Kulkarni

Walchand College of Engineering, Sangli, MH, India
{siddheshwar.patil,dinesh.kulkarni}@walchandsangli.ac.in

Abstract. Data is growing. The growth is twofold – size and dimensionality. To deal with such a huge data – "the big data", researchers, data analysts are relying on the machine learning and data mining techniques. However, the performance of these techniques is degrading due to this twofold growth that further adds to the complexity of the data. The need of the hour is to leave up with the complexity of such a datasets and to focus on improving the accuracy of data mining and machine learning techniques as well as on enhancing the performance of the algorithms. The accuracy of the mining algorithms can be enhanced by reducing dimensionality of data. Not all information that contributes to the dimensionality of the datasets is important for the said techniques of data analysis – the dimensionality can be reduced. Contemporary research focuses on the techniques of removing unwanted, unnecessary, redundant information; importantly removing the data that adds up to dimensionality making it high dimensional. The performance of the algorithm is further upgraded with the help of the parallel computing on high-performance computing (HPC) infrastructure. Parallel computing on multi-core and many-core architectures, on the low-cost general purpose graphics processing unit (GPGPU) is a boon for data analysts, researchers for finding high-performance solutions. The GPGPU have gained popularity due to their cost benefits and very high data processing power. Also, parallel processing techniques achieve better speedup and scaleup. The objective of this paper is to present an insight for the researchers, data analysts on how the high dimensionality of the data can be dealt with so that the accuracy and computational complexity of the machine learning and data mining techniques is not compromised. To prove the point, this work discusses various parallel computing approaches on multi-core (CPU) and many-core architectures (GPGPU) for time complexity enhancement. Moreover, the contemporary dimensionality reduction methods are reviewed.

Keywords: High-performance computing · Parallel computing · Dimensionality reduction · Classification · High-dimensionality data · General purpose graphics processing unit

© Springer Nature Singapore Pte Ltd. 2019
A. Majumdar and R. Arora (Eds.): SCEC 2018, CCIS 964, pp. 54–63, 2019.
https://doi.org/10.1007/978-981-13-7729-7_4

1   Introduction

Dimensionality of a dataset is a number of attributes of a dataset. For example, medical data has blood pressure, weight, cholesterol level, etc. as its attributes. When number of attributes is over, say 100, such a dataset is a High Dimensional dataset. For high dimensional data, the number of attributes is greater than the sample sizes. The calculations on such a staggeringly high number of attributes become extremely difficult. The high dimensionality data is generated at an extraordinary rate from different sources, viz., data from social networks, geological data, healthcare data, ecological data, data originating from government agencies etc. This is evident from the literature survey - in libSVM database, in year 1990s, the maximum dimensionality stood almost 62,000; it increased to 16 million in first decade of the current century. It has, now, in the current decade reached to almost 29 million [1–3]. On such a "big data", the present learning algorithms do not always operate in an appropriately suitable way. This has become a challenge for the data analysts, researchers to work on high dimensionality dataset. High dimensional dataset reduces performance of the training algorithm since the algorithm attempts to use all the features in that dataset. Thus, to operate on such a "big data", it is necessary to decrease the dimensionality. In dimensionality reduction, the "extra information" is reduced and only significant features are retained eliminating the unnecessary, redundant data. Decrease in dimension of the dataset increases the accuracy of classification and thus decreases the computational cost of a classification algorithm. The computational complexity (time and space) is more for the traditional classification methods operating on high dimensional data. For such numerous computational problems, algorithms based on CPU are far behind from matching the expectations. Additionally, with growing size of data and dimensionality, the CPU algorithms based on multi-cores are becoming inadequate. To achieve the desired results for such a computation intensive problems – involving high dimensionality of the data – we require many-core architectures [4]. It is a need of the hour to employ high-performance parallel computing approaches to match the computational requirements of learning algorithms.

2   Dimensionality Reduction

Dimensionality reduction is a method of mapping data from high-dimensional set to lower-dimensional set. It is a technique to convert data having enormous dimensions into reduced dimensions ensuring that it carries similar information. The performance of classification affects because of noise, redundant or irrelevant attributes in the data. So, dimension reduction is necessary to perform preprocessing on training data to achieve good results.

PCA algorithm [5] shows the mapping of original data model to diverse degrees. i.e. It carries distance relations of data by projecting it orthogonally onto linear subspace which have target dimensionality. Then it learns the principal components (linearly un-correlated features) which define variance term of data. Dimensionality reduction is done by showing given input data through principal component subsets which will describe best variance of data. PCA minimizes least square error for Euclidean distances in data and target space by maximizing the variance. Attributes having minimum involvement to variances is measured as less descriptive. These attributes will be removed.

The PCA does not require labels; it is unsupervised while linear discriminant analysis (LDA) is supervised. It is similar to PCA. The LDA will not increase variance but it creates linear surfaces to distinct groups. LDA finds the vectors on underlying space. They must be discriminate among different classes. Furthermore, LDA produces major mean differences among desired classes. It generates linear combination, if distinct features are available specific to subject. For samples from various classes, there can be two defined parameters in which first is within-class scatter matrix and next is between-class scatter matrix. Objective function is to decrease within-class distance measure whereas improve between-class measure.

NMF [6] decomposes non-negative matrix to product of two non-negative ones. It is a favorable tool wherever simply non-negative signals exists like in astronomy. It divides the input data to two parts. One is positive basis matrix while another is positive coefficient matrix. From data, the commonly occurring parts are learned by Positive basis matrix. To show the reconstructed commonly occurring data parts, positive coefficient matrix is used. NMF accomplishes reduction of dimensions by selecting data from positive basis matrix. NMF retains data parts that are commonly occurring parts whereas deletes the rarely occurring parts of data.

In Random projection (RP) [7], the unique d-dimensional dataset will be converted into k-dimensional ($k \ll d$) subspace by a random $k * d$ matrix R. RP does projecting of data to lower k-dimensional space. The Johnson-lindenstrauss lemma is used for random mapping. The points from vector space will be projected to the subspaces (randomly selected) of appropriate high dimensions and then distance among points will be roughly preserved. RP has low computational cost.

Autoencoder (AE) [8–10] is powerful method which reduces dimensionality of huge data. It is based on neural network. It may feed-forward, recurrent or convolutional, many of architectures are adjusted into an autoencoder which tries to learn the input. It has equal output and input data. When input layer neurons are more than hidden layer neurons then reduction is performed. Linear Auto Encoding is similar to PCA which learns variance information. Nonlinear Auto-Encoder learns non-linear features.

Multidimensional scaling (MDS) [11] achieves a lower dimensional representation of data by keeping constant distances between data points. The method is known as distance method. Distance is used as similarity or dissimilarity measure.

Locally Linear Embedding (LLE) [12] addresses problem of nonlinearity. From high-dimensional data, it computes the low-dimensional, neighborhood preserving embedding. A data set of n dimension will be mapped to a lower dimension d which will be close to nonlinear manifold of dimensionality $d < n$. The local linear fits helps to improve global nonlinear structure.

The nonlinear technique, Isomap [13] takes geodesic interpoint distances as an alternative for Euclidean distances. Shortest paths with curved surface of manifold are obtained by using geodesic distances. For complex natural observations, Isomap discovers nonlinear degrees of freedom. The learning method based on Extreme Learning Machine (ELM) are efficient for regression and classification [14]. It has number of dimensionality mapping functions such as Gaussian, sigmoid, multi-quadratic, Fourier series, wavelet etc. It has power to handle both large and small datasets in efficient way. For high-dimensional datasets, before using K-nearest neighbor algorithm (k-NN) [15] dimension reduction is performed to get good results.

3   Literature Review

Yamada, Tang et al. [1] proposed a nonlinear feature selection from ultra high-dimensional big biological and medical data. They discovered complex nonlinear relationships using machine learning methods. As the traditional learning methods are computationally impracticable for dataset having million features. Authors introduced dimensionality reduction technique which can scale for ultra-high dimensional data for nonlinear learning problems. It uses Hilbert-Schmidt Independence Criterion (HSIC) with Lasso to deal with thousands samples with million features. It finds optimal set having high predictive features with minimum redundancy which yields high interpretability and predictive power. Authors achieved better accuracy to select 20 features from one million features (dimensionality reduction up to 99.98%). The algorithms are implemented on apache spark platform.

As the hyperspectral data usually consists of redundancy which can be eliminated using dimensionality reduction. Wu, Li et al. [2] presented a technique for dimensionality reduction on cloud computing environments having proficient storage and preprocessing capacity of data. They created a parallel and distributed version of PCA and uses cloud computing platform. The execution uses file system of Hadoop as a distributed storage and computing engine as apache spark. It uses parallel map-reduce model. So, they shown benefit of both distributed HPC abilities of cloud computing environment and high throughput access. They also showed optimization in traditional PCA which is finest for parallel and distributed computing. Further, it is implemented on actual cloud computing architecture. The result for the proposed parallel method on numerous hyperspectral datasets shows high performance.

Ramirez-Gallego, Lastra et al. [3] have presented a maximum relevance and minimum redundancy (mRMR) method for dimensionality reduction. Authors have used Apache Spark to accelerate the performance efficiency and accuracy. The proposed method gives high accuracy, so called to be the most relevant method for dimensionality reduction but having computationally expensive as it deals with many features. Authors present fast-mRMR that minimizes this computational load. Along the fast-mRMR, authors showcased implementations of their algorithm, specifically, sequential execution on CPU, parallel computing on GPGPU, and distributed computing on apache spark. The results shows that parallel implementation (GPGPU) are best than sequential (CPU) in cases when there are large number of records (>100, 000 approximately). Results also shows that spark is the better than CPU version for high number of features ≥2000 roughly). Authors suggested possible future research on dimensionality reduction of high-speed data streams and developing automatic system which filters most appropriate set of attributes (features), thus removing the requirement to provide the number of features at every execution.

Martel, Lazcano et al. [4] proposed a dimensionality reduction by PCA to raise the performance and effectiveness of wide hyperspectral image algorithms. They have shown the execution of PCA on high-performance infrastructures such as GPGPU from NVIDIA and Kalray many-core. They have shown full utilization of the HPC infrastructure which will help to reduces the time needed for processing of a given hyperspectral images. Furthermore, the experimental results are compared with results obtained using PCA on field programmable gate array (FPGA). According to results, dimensionality reduction by PCA on GPGPU outperforms the FPGA based method.

Zubova, Liutvinavicius, Kurasov [16] presented a Random Projection to minimize dimensionality of data. They shown experiments on how parallel computing using OpenMP and MPI technologies can enhance performance of dimensionality reduction method. Their result shows that, there is significant performance improvement when executing Message Passing Interface (MPI) program on cluster. Authors further says that, increase in number of cores not always leads to optimal speed.

Due to high-dimensionality, huge-volume and low-quality of economic data pose challenges on efficient economic big data analysis. When deals with large varieties of economic factors, learning methods yields poor performance. By considering the challenges, Zhao, Chen et al. [17] proposed a method to efficiently analyze high-dimensional big economic data using distributed feature selection technique. In this, it first reduces noise, cleans and transforms the data using preprocessing and normalization. Afterward a distributed subtractive clustering method is presented to build a two-layer feature selection model, which selects significant features and identifies the representative ones of economic big data. The proposed algorithms uses MapReduce framework. The experimentation performed on the economic data and their result shows that the proposed methods and framework have greater performance in analyzing enormous data.

Cuomo, Galletti et al. [18] presented Singular Value Decomposition (SVD) dimensionality reduction technique to process high-dimensional data. It gains fuzzy-rough reduced converge for higher dimensional data. Though SVD has good properties, the computational cost is still an issue. Authors presented a parallel version of SVD using CUDA programming on GPGPU. Result shows the significant performance improvement as compared to CPU version for expensive processing of data.

Tang, Yu et al. [19] proposed a parallel approach on high dimensional data for skyline query processing. On the multidimensional data points, the skyline query retrieves points which should not come under any other point from set. Because of pervasive usage of skyline queries, there are many challenges that are still not addressed. Authors introduced a novel efficient approach for running the skyline queries on a large-scale data. In this work, the data is firstly partitioned with z-order curve. To reduce dimensions of intermediate data, it takes the optimization problem as a data partitioning. Secondly, every computational node partitions input data to distinct sets. Further it implements parallel skyline computation on each distinct set. At last, indexes are built and uses the efficient method to combine the produced skyline candidates. Several implementations show that skyline code gains better performance improvement as compared to existing approaches.

Passi, Nour and Jain [20] explained a technique to identify genes for analysis of microarray expression using clinical behavior from cancer datasets. It finds significant genes using Markov blanket algorithm. Authors compared performance of Markov blanket-based model with various wrapper based dimensionality (genes) reduction approaches on various microarray datasets. The wrapper-based approach depends on memetic algorithms. For the Markov blanket, they have used minimum redundant maximum relevance dimensionality reduction optimized with genetic algorithms. They have done performance comparison of the Markov blanket method with other classifiers using same set of features. Performance of Markov blanket classification algorithm shows best accuracy than existing methods for cancer microarray datasets.

Li, Zhang, Zhang et al. [21] presented a novel isometric mapping (ISOMAP) from linear projection methods to reduce dimensions of hyperspectral images (HSI). Considering nonlinear mapping, it represents features to a low-dimensional set by preserving the local structure of original dataset. So, it benefits for data analysis. Since computational cost is very high for HSI learning algorithm. Some parallel implementations are available but they are not able to accelerate eigen-decomposition process which is most time-consuming part in ISOMAP algorithm. In this paper, authors implemented ISOMAP algorithm on graphics processing unit. In particular, authors focused on eigen-decomposition processing. The experimentation result obtained on HSI dataset shows excellent speedup without affecting accuracy of the classification as compared to its sequential implementation.

The summary of some literature reviewed in this paper is reported in Table 1 and few high dimensional datasets [22, 23] are listed in Table 2.

4   Challenges

We found following challenges during review of literature.

1. The high dimensional data is having special characteristic such as data with huge number of attributes or features. So, it is challenging work to select

Table 1. Summary of dimensionality reduction algorithm, parallel programming model, H/W configuration and datasets

Author	Dimensionality reduction algorithm	Parallel programming model	H/W configuration	Datasets
Yamada et al. [1]	Hilbert-schmidt independence criterion lasso with least angle regression (LAND)	MapReduce framework (hadoop and apache spark)	Intel xeon 2.4 GHz, 24 GB RAM (16 cores)	P53, Enzyme
Wu et al. [2]	Principal component analysis	MapReduce framework (hadoop and apache spark), MPI Cluster	Cloud computing (Intel Xeon E5630 CPUs (8 cores) 2.53 GHz, 5GB RAM, 292 GB SAS HDD), 8 slave (Intel Xeon E7-4807 CPUs (12 cores) 1.86 GHz)	AVIRIS cuprite hyperspectral datasets
Ramirez-Gallego et al. [3]	Minimum redundancy maximum relevance (mRMR)	MapReduce on apache spark, CUDA on GPGPU	Cluster (18 computing nodes, 1 master node) computing nodes: Intel Xeon E5-2620, 6 cores/processor, 64 GB RAM	Epsilon, URL, Kddb
Martel et al. [4]	Principal component analysis	CUDA on GPGPU	Intel core i7-4790, NVIDIA 32 GB Memory, GeForce GTX 680 GPU	Hyperspectral data
Zubova et al. [16]	Random projection	MPI Cluster	-	URL, Kddb
Zhao et al. [17]	Distributed subtractive clustering	Cluster platforms	-	Economic data (China)
Cuomo et al. [18]	Singular value decomposition	CUDA on GPGPU	Intel core i7, 8 GB RAM, 2.8 GHz, GPU NVIDIA Quadro K5000, 1536 CUDA cores	-
Li et al. [21]	Isometric mapping (ISOMAP)	CUDA on GPGPU	Intel core i7-4790, 3.6 GHz, 8 cores, 32 GB RAM GPU- Nvidia GTX 1080, 2560 CUDA cores, 8 GB RAM	HSI datasets-Indian pines, Salinas, Pavia

suitable, relevant set of features for attaining the best accurate results for classification.

2. From high dimensionality dataset, selecting appropriate features is a time-consuming process. The time and space cost of learning feature selection/classification algorithms is large and grows fast as the variables increases.

3. The existing methods for high dimensional data are not working appropriately in an efficient way. Therefore, reducing data complexity is challenging for data analysis, knowledge inference algorithms.

4. Since, feature extraction algorithms such as PCA, kPCA "blend" the existing dimensions to create new ones. For example, the rotation of data in conventional PCA reorients the data so that the new set of dimensions is a linear combination of initial given dimensions, leaving the less useful parts of each dimension to be omitted. Feature extraction, therefore, can be more complex.

Table 2. Summary description of some high-dimensional datasets

Data set	Instances	Dimensions	Classes
Brain tumor	50	10367	4
Colon	62	2000	2
Leukemia	47	2000	2
Lymphomas	77	5470	2
DNA	79739293	200	2
Epsilon	400000	2000	2
URL	1916904	3231961	2
ECBDL14	65003913	630	2
Kddb	19264097	29890095	2

5. There exists commonly used dimensionality reduction techniques like information gain, mutual information, chi-square which are depends upon pairwise statistics. They will not work well if the training data is small in size.
6. New technique such as Markov blanket bayesian network is introduced for dimensionality reduction. Markov blanket is best suitable for dimensionality reduction from datasets because of strong dependency characteristic among features. For Markov blanket learning, space and time cost is large. It grows fast as the variable size get increases. Also, for its independence test, huge data is required which makes the problem harder.

5   Parallel Computing Approaches

From the literature reviews discussed in this paper, the computing approaches for high dimensional data are categorized based on distributed and shared memory platforms. GPGPU is a shared memory model and MapReduce is distributed computing framework. They can be used for horizontal and vertical scaling. HPC cluster (MPI), GPGPU can be used for vertical scaling purpose. Hadoop and apache spark can be used for horizontal scaling purpose. Vertical scaling increases the computational power, resources, and memory requirement of every node from the system. In horizontal scaling, it will make addition of new nodes in the system and distributes the work among them.

Since, MapReduce frameworks are not properly suit for iterative algorithms because their launch overhead performance is very less. The new jobs creation, nodes synchronization and data transfers makes an overhead. So, distributed frameworks are not suitable for learning process. Also, jobs run independently which makes it difficult to implement shared communication within intermediate processes. it needs a fault-tolerant Hadoop distributed file system (HDFS). Many researchers are using apache spark as an alternative to MapReduce Hadoop. Apache spark runs the application 100 times fast in memory and 10 times fast in disk than MapReduce Hadoop framework. Since, spark decreases number of write and read cycles to disk as it stores intermediate data in memory. The kernel launch overhead of GPGPU is very small which will help to execute parallel tasks without delay and obtain the fast results. As the massive parallelism is provided by GPGPU for big scale machine learning tasks, the algorithms can scale for data volume which is not computable by sequential algorithms. Multi-GPGPU and distributed-GPGPU can combine hardware resources to solve scaling problem for bigger data. Spark workload can also be accelerated using GPGPU.

6   Conclusion

This paper presents an insight for the researchers, data analysts on how the high dimensionality data problems can be solved using data dimension reduction techniques and the GPGPU, MPI Cluster, OpenMP and Apache Spark based infrastructures. It mentions the challenges, difficulties with the high dimensionality and state of the art dimensionality reduction techniques for solving these difficulties. The importance of the parallel computing techniques based on the data and computational requirements is discussed. Subsequently, the high-performance computing approaches that can be employed to solve the problems with the high dimensional data are described. For high dimensional data, the low cost and high-performance GPGPU infrastructure can be effectively used to gain performance benefits. However, if the scalability of the "big data" becomes limited due to the GPGPU memory capacity then multi-GPGPU and cluster-computing framework like MPI and spark can be used. It appears that combining multiple platforms, techniques mentioned above shall be more suitable to solve the challenges with high dimensionality data. For example, combination of spark with GPGPU is gaining better speedup in proportion to scaleup.

References

1. Yamada, M., et al.: Ultra high-dimensional nonlinear feature selection for big biological data. IEEE Trans. Knowl. Data Eng. **30**(7), 1352–1365 (2018)
2. Wu, Z., Li, Y., Plaza, A., Li, J., Xiao, F., Wei, Z.: Parallel and distributed dimensionality reduction of hyperspectral data on cloud computing architectures. IEEE J. Sel. Top. Appl. Earth Obs. Remote Sens. **9**(6), 2270–2278 (2016)
3. Ramírez-Gallego, S., et al.: An information theory-based feature selection framework for big data under apache spark. IEEE Trans. Syst. Man Cybern. Syst. **48**(9), 1441–1453 (2018)
4. Martel, E., et al.: Implementation of the principal component analysis onto high-performance computer facilities for hyperspectral dimensionality reduction: results and comparisons. Remote Sens. **10**(6), 864 (2018)
5. Hotelling, H.: Analysis of a complex of statistical variables into principal components. J. Educ. Psychol. **24**(6), 417 (1933)
6. Lee, D.D., Seung, H.S.: Learning the parts of objects by non-negative matrix factorization. Nature **401**(6755), 788 (1999)
7. Achlioptas, D.: Database-friendly random projections. In: Proceedings of the Twentieth ACM SIGMOD-SIGACT-SIGART Symposium on Principles of Database Systems, pp. 274–281. ACM (2001)

8. Bengio, Y., et al.: Learning deep architectures for AI. Found. Trends® Mach. Learn. **2**(1), 1–127 (2009)
9. Bengio, Y., Courville, A., Vincent, P.: Representation learning: a review and new perspectives. IEEE Trans. Pattern Anal. Mach. Intell. **35**(8), 1798–1828 (2013)
10. Chen, M., Xu, Z., Weinberger, K., Sha, F.: Marginalized denoising autoencoders for domain adaptation. arXiv preprint arXiv:1206.4683 (2012)
11. Cox, T.F., Cox, M.A.: Multidimensional Scaling. Chapman and Hall/CRC, Boca Raton (2000)
12. Roweis, S.T., Saul, L.K.: Nonlinear dimensionality reduction by locally linear embedding. Science **290**(5500), 2323–2326 (2000)
13. Tenenbaum, J.B., De Silva, V., Langford, J.C.: A global geometric framework for nonlinear dimensionality reduction. Science **290**(5500), 2319–2323 (2000)
14. Kasun, L.L.C., Yang, Y., Huang, G.B., Zhang, Z.: Dimension reduction with extreme learning machine. IEEE Trans. Image Process. **25**(8), 3906–3918 (2016)
15. Beyer, K., Goldstein, J., Ramakrishnan, R., Shaft, U.: When is "nearest neighbor" meaningful? In: Beeri, C., Buneman, P. (eds.) ICDT 1999. LNCS, vol. 1540, pp. 217–235. Springer, Heidelberg (1999). https://doi.org/10.1007/3-540-49257-7_15
16. Zubova, J., Liutvinavicius, M., Kurasova, O.: Parallel computing for dimensionality reduction. In: Dregvaite, G., Damasevicius, R. (eds.) ICIST 2016. CCIS, vol. 639, pp. 230–241. Springer, Cham (2016). https://doi.org/10.1007/978-3-319-46254-7_19
17. Zhao, L., Chen, Z., Hu, Y., Min, G., Jiang, Z.: Distributed feature selection for efficient economic big data analysis. IEEE Trans. Big Data **2**, 164–176 (2018)
18. Cuomo, S., Galletti, A., Marcellino, L., Navarra, G., Toraldo, G.: On GPU-CUDA as preprocessing of fuzzy-rough data reduction by means of singular value decomposition. Soft Comput. **22**(5), 1525–1532 (2018)
19. Tang, M., Yu, Y., Aref, W.G., Malluhi, Q., Ouzzani, M.: Efficient parallel skyline query processing for high-dimensional data. IEEE Trans. Knowl. Data Eng. **30**, 1838–1851 (2018)
20. Passi, K., Nour, A., Jain, C.K.: Markov blanket: efficient strategy for feature subset selection method for high dimensional microarray cancer datasets. In: 2017 IEEE International Conference on Bioinformatics and Biomedicine (BIBM), pp. 1864–1871. IEEE (2017)
21. Li, W., Zhang, L., Zhang, L., Du, B.: GPU parallel implementation of isometric mapping for hyperspectral classification. IEEE Geosci. Remote Sens. Lett. **14**(9), 1532–1536 (2017)
22. Dheeru, D., Taniskidou, E.K.: UCI machine learning repository (2017). http://archive.ics.uci.edu/ml
23. Hyperspectral dataset. http://lesun.weebly.com/hyperspectral-data-set.html

Performance Analysis and Optimization

Performance Analysis of Computational Neuroscience Software NEURON on Knights Corner Many Core Processors

Pramod S. Kumbhar[2], Subhashini Sivagnanam[1],
Kenneth Yoshimoto[1], Michael Hines[3], Ted Carnevale[3],
and Amit Majumdar[1(✉)]

[1] San Diego Supercomputer Center, University of California San Diego,
San Diego, CA 92039, USA
`majumdar@sdsc.edu`
[2] Ecole Polytechnique Fédérale de Lausanne, 1015 Laussanne, Switzerland
[3] Neuroscience Department, Yale University, New Haven, CT 06520, USA

Abstract. In this paper we analyze the performance of the computational neuroscience tool NEURON on Intel Knights Corner processors. Knights Corner was the many core processor that was followed by Knights Landing processors. NEURON is a widely used simulation environment for modeling individual neurons and network of neurons. NEURON is used to simulate large models requiring high performance computing, and understanding performance of NEURON on many core processors is of interest to the neuroscience community, as well as to the high performance computing community. NEURON supports parallelization using Message Passing Interface (MPI) library. Parallel performance of NEURON has been analyzed on various types of high performance resources. We analyze the performance and load balance of NEURON for two different size problems on Knights Corner. We use the TAU and Vampir tool to analyze load imbalance issues of these runs. We compare performance on the host SandyBridge processors of Knights Corner versus on the Many Integrated Core (MIC) cores of Knights Corner.

Keywords: Knights Corner · NEURON · Load balance

1 Introduction

In this paper we analyze performance of the widely used computational neuroscience tool NEURON [1, 2] on Intel's Knights Corner coprocessors. As a part of the US BRAIN Initiative [3] and EU Human Brain Project [4], both of which started in 2013, there is tremendous interest and effort among neuroscientists for large scale neuronal models with the goal towards understanding how the brain functions both in normal and diseased conditions. The goal of the US BRAIN Initiative, a joint effort by NIH, NSF, DARPA, IARPA, DOD, FDA and private organizations, is to show for the first time how individual cells and complex neural circuits interact in both time and space. This will lead to treating, curing and even preventing brain disorders such as Alzheimer's disease, Parkinson's disease, autism, epilepsy, depression and traumatic

© Springer Nature Singapore Pte Ltd. 2019
A. Majumdar and R. Arora (Eds.): SCEC 2018, CCIS 964, pp. 67–76, 2019.
https://doi.org/10.1007/978-981-13-7729-7_5

brain injury. The EU Human Brain Project (HBP) is a collaborative effort to simulate the brain within a decade and along the way map all the neurons and synapses to help build a computer model of the brain. Using that model scientists can learn more about human thoughts as well as neurological diseases. HPC and simulations are big part of the HBP.

Performance of large scale neuronal models on different types of high performance computing (HPC) resources is an active field of research among computational neuroscientists and computer scientists. As is known by neuroscientists the human brain consists of about 100 billion neurons and about 100 trillion synapses. To give a perspective of the importance of HPC for computational neuroscience, Table 1 provides a list of some of the largest scale neuronal simulations that have been attempted by various groups to date. In the last row of Table 1, we provide the perspective of need for exascale computing for neuroscientists if attempt is going to be made to model the whole human brain. This is a very qualitative and simple perspective of exascale for modeling the human brain – i.e. if for ~ 1 billion neurons and ~ 10 trillion synapses ~ 10 petaflop is used (see Table 1, Diesmann group and others) [5–7] then for 100 billion neurons and 100 trillion synapses ~ 100X of 10 petaflop would be needed i.e. of the scale of exascale computing.

Table 1. Large scale HPC neuronal simulations.

Research group, year	Neuronal simulation on HPC resource
European Human Brain Project, 2013	6 PF machine, 450 TB memory system can simulate 100 million cells $\sim$ Mouse brain
Michael Hines (Yale U.) et al., 2011	32 million cells and up to 32 billion connections using 128,000 BlueGene/P cores
Ananthanarayanan et al., 2009; IBM group	1.6 billion neurons and 8.87 trillion synapses experimentally-measured gray matter thalamocortical connectivity using 147,456 CPUs, 144 TB of memory BlueGene/P
Diesmann and group 2014–2015; Institute for Advanced Simulations & JARA Brain Institute, Research Center Jülich; Department of Physics, RWTH Aachen University, Germany	1.86 billion neurons with 11 trillion synapses on the K computer (~ 10 petaflop peak machine, Japan) using 82,944 processors, 1 PB of memory
Exascale for neuroscientists? 2022–2024?	*About 100 billion neurons and about 100 trillion synapses – Exascale computing*

Knights Corner (KNC) is part of Intel's x86 manycore processors. It is meant to be used in supercomputers, servers and high-end workstations. Its architecture allows standard programming languages and APIs such as MPI and OpenMP. It was available for the user community on the first Stampede machine at the Texas Advanced Computing Center (TACC) at the University of Texas at Austin. It was also available at EU centers such as the Juelich Supercomputer Center in Germany. The Stampede architecture details of KNC and E5 processors, used for running the NEURON benchmark, is given in reference [8]. Here we highlight some of its higher level features. KNC has 61 Xeon Phi SE10P with clock speed of 1.1 GHz and each KNC coprocessor had 8 GB of GDDR5 memory. It has Intel x86 architecture and runs Linux OS. MPI tasks can be run on the 61 cores along with MPI tasks running on the host E5 processors. On the Stampede KNC nodes there was two 8-core Xeon E5 host processors, with clock speed of 2.7 GHz and 2 GB/core memory resulting total of 32 GB/node. The 16 E5 cores provided peak performance of 346 GFlops and the 61 KNC cores provided peak of about 1 TFlops.

2   NEURON

The operation of biological neural systems involves the propagation and interaction of electrical and chemical signals that are distributed in space and time. NEURON is designed to be useful as a tool for understanding how nervous system function emerges from the properties of biological neurons and networks. It is particularly well-suited for models of neurons and neural circuits that are closely linked to experimental obser- vations and involve complex anatomical and biophysical properties, electrical and/or chemical signaling. It us used by experimental and computation neuroscientists worldwide. It is used for the analysis of cellular mechanism underlying and evaluation of pharmacological methods for neurological disorders, research on mechanisms involved in progression of neurodegenerative diseases, preclinical evaluation of potential psychotherapeutic drugs, and design of electrodes and simulation protocols in deep brain or spinal cord simulation for treatment.

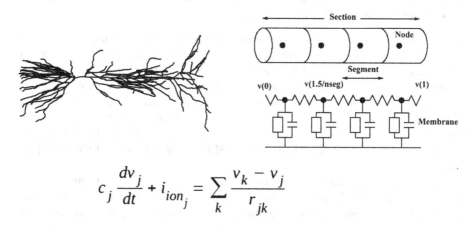

$$c_j \frac{dv_j}{dt} + i_{ion_j} = \sum_k \frac{v_k - v_j}{r_{jk}}$$

Fig. 1. A description of NEURON setup for modeling.

As shown in Fig. 1, each branch (top left in Fig. 1) of a cell is represented by one or more compartments (top right in Fig. 1). Each compartment is described by a family of differential equations (bottom of Fig. 1). Each compartment's net ionic current i_{ion_j} is the sum of one or more currents that may themselves be governed by one or more differential equations. A single cell may be represented by many thousands of equations.

In NEURON, parallel simulation of cells and networks may use combination of multithreaded execution, bulletin-board-style execution for embarrassingly parallel problems and execution of a model that is distributed over multiple tasks on cores using MPI. Complex models can be carefully split and distribute over multiple cores for load balance.

3   Porting and Performance Analysis on KNC

We used the following machines where a NEURON model was ported and ran for analyzing and comparing performance.

Texas Advanced Computing Center's – TACC (USA) Stampede machine
- SandyBridge dual socket, two 8 cores/socket Xeon E5-2680 processors, 2.7 GHz, 32 GB/node
- Xeon KNC-MIC SE10P Coprocessors, 61 cores, 1.1 GHz with 8 GB of memory
- Mellanox Inifiniband FDR interconnect

Juelich Supercomputer Center – JCC (Germany) KNL-MIC cluster
- Dual socket, two 8 cores/socket SandyBridge processors, 2.6 GHz; 16 GB/node
- Xeon KNC coprocessors, 61 cores, 1.23 GHz with 1 GB memory
- Mellanox Inifiniband FDR interconnect

San Diego Supercomputer Center – SDSC (USA) Comet machine
- Dual socket, two 12 cores/socket E5-2680v3 Haswell, 2.5 GHz; 128 GB/node
- Mellanox Infiniband FDR interconnect

We used the popular Jones Model [9] developed by the research group of Stephanie Jones from Brown University, USA for performance analysis using the NEURON software. Details of the model is provide in the reference [9]. It is a biophysically principled computational neural model of the primary somatosensory cortex (SI), with distinct laminae, inhibitory and excitatory neurons, and feedforward (FF, representative of lemniscal thalamic drive) and feedback (FB, representative of higher-order cortical drive or input from nonlemniscal thalamic nuclei) inputs defined by the laminar location of their postsynaptic effects. It uses MPI for parallelization of the NEURON model.

Table 2 shows the timing results on Stampede SandyBridge and Comet Haswell [10] processors for the Jones model with about 300 neuron cells of two different types (pyramidal neurons and single compartment inhibitory neurons). The timing behavior is as expected on these two processors when clock speed and memory bandwidth and interconnects are taken into account (both Stampede and Comet have Infiniband FDR interconnects).

Table 2. Timing of Jones model (~ 300 neurons) on Haswell (SDSC) and SandyBridge (TACC).

# of Comet Haswell cores	Timing (sec)
1	211
4	51
8	27
16	15
24	11
# of Stampede SandyBridge cores	Timing (sec)
1	269
4	57
8	27
16	14

Table 3 shows the timing of the Jones model run on Stampede where the runs use MPI tasks on both SandyBridge cores and KNC cores. Multiple runs were made for each case and the timing range shows the variations in timing that we observed from run to run on the SandyBridge and the KNC cores. We observed bit more variations in timing on the KNC cores from run to run. It is possible that this is due to load imbalance as we discuss in the later part of this paper.

Table 3. Timing of Jones model on Stampede SandyBridge and KNC-MIC cores.

# of CPU cores	# of KNC cores	Timing (sec) (run to run timing variations)
16	8	342 (~ 7–~ 9 s CPU; ~ 303–~ 324 s KNC)
16	16	264 (~ 5–~ 7 s CPU; ~ 218–~ 242 s KNC)
16	32	162 (~ 3–~ 5 s CPU; ~ 150–~ 139 s KNC)
16	60	129 (~ 3 s CPU; ~ 67–~ 87–~ 123 s KNC)
8	8	497 (~ 13 s CPU; ~ 478–~ 488 s KNC)
8	16	358 (~ 9 s CPU; ~ 304–~ 317 s KNC)
8	32	211 (~ 5 s CPU; ~ 160–~ 200 s KNC)
8	60	130 (~ 3 s CPU; ~ 67–~ 80–~ 120 s KNC)

Figures 2 and 3 show the performance plots of Jones model for 100 neuron cells (in 2-dimensional grid with 10 cells in X dimension and 10 cells in Y dimension) on the Jülich Supercomputer Center's machine with SandyBridge (host) and KNC-MIC coprocessor. The test case was run for 150 time steps. Multiple MPI ranks are used on each core. We see that KNC-MIC is (best timing of 5.8 s; Fig. 3) 3.8X slower than SandyBridge (best timing of 1.5 s; Fig. 2) for this 100 neuron cells test case.

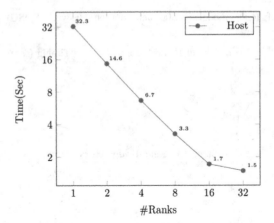

Fig. 2. Jones Model (100 cells) timing on Jülich SandyBridge host.

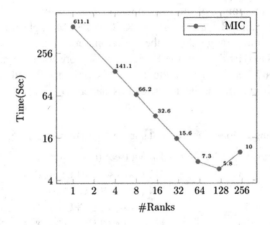

Fig. 3. Jones Model (100 cells) timing on Jülich machine KNC-MIC co-processor.

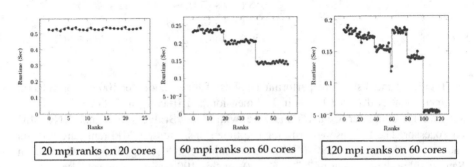

Fig. 4. Load balance analysis on KNC-MIC.

Figure 4 shows runtime comparison on KNC while using different number of ranks/cores. Runtime is well balanced for the first case (Fig. 4 Left) but there is high variation as we increase number of ranks/cores (Fig. 4 Center and Right).

To understand this timing we analyzed the results using the TAU tracing tool [11] and visualized using Vampir [12] as shown in Fig. 5. We see that load imbalance increases with increase of MPI ranks/core i.e. 100 neuron cells are not distribute evenly across MPI tasks. This tells us that in order to utilize all the 60 KNC-MIC cores we need to use a larger model with more cells.

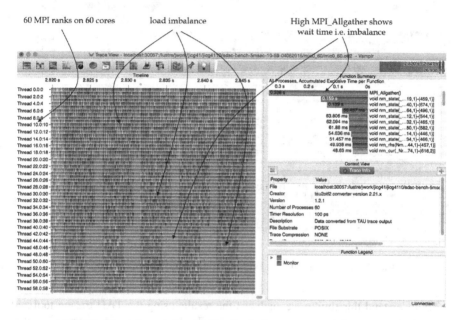

Fig. 5. Tracing analysis of 100 cells timing case on Jülich machine.

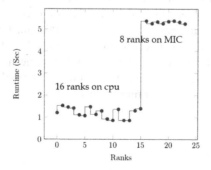

Fig. 6. Hybrid host and KNC-MIC timing case on Jülich machine.

Figure 6 shows timing analysis of a hybrid run where timings on both SandyBridge (16 ranks on CPU) and KNC-MIC (8 ranks on KNC-MIC) are shown. MPI ranks on SandyBridge take lot less time than on the MPI ranks on the KNC-MIC and this is expected as KNC cores are slower compared to SandyBridge cores.

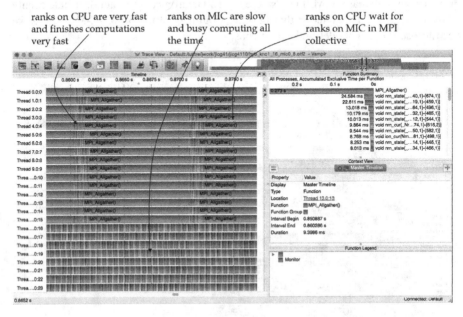

Fig. 7. Tracing result of hybrid case run (corresponding to Fig. 6).

To understand this timing we analyzed the results using the TAU tracing tool and visualized using Vampir as shown in Fig. 7. This shows, as expected, that SandyBridge CPU cores are faster and complete computation before KNC-MIC cores and wait for KNC-MIC cores to catch up.

Currently NEURON distributes equal amount of work to all the MPI tasks i.e. to the tasks on the SandyBridge cores and the KNC-MIC cores. Considering that the SandyBridge cores are faster than KNC-MIC cores, this equal distribution of work is not suitable for weaker KNC-MIC cores from the point of load balance.

This first analysis provided us with the insight that we need to run a larger problem to deal with load imbalance. Next runs were done for a problem that has 480 cells (compared to 100 cells for the earlier runs) with 48 cells in X dimension and 10 cells in Y dimension.

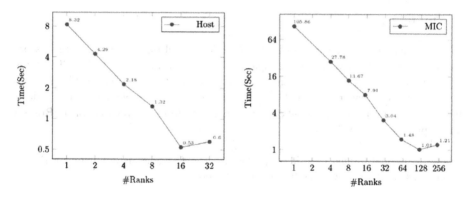

Fig. 8. Larger problem size (480 cells) results on host and KNC-MIC.

Figure 8 shows that for the larger problem size the performance on KNC-MIC improves as the load balance is better. As a result KNC-MIC (best time 1.03 s; right figure of Fig. 8) is now only 1.9X slower than SandyBridge (best time 0.53 s; left figure of Fig. 8). We performed tracing with TAU for this case also and the Vampir visualization of TAU results are shown in Fig. 9. Results from Fig. 9 show that there is very little MPI_Allgather wait time for this larger problem case compared to the smaller problem case as was observed in Fig. 5. Having more cells (480 compare to 100 for the earlier case) allowed each MPI task (i.e. MPI tasks both on SandyBridge and on KNC-MIC) to have similar amount of computational work.

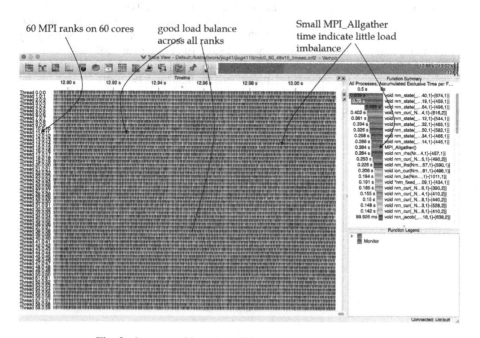

Fig. 9. Larger problem size (480 cells) TAU tracing results.

4 Summary

We analyzed Jones model run using the NEURON tool on regular Xeon processors (SandyBridge and Haswell). We compared performance on SandyBridge CPU cores with performance on KNC-MIC coprocessors. The results show that load balance on large number of weaker KNC-MIC cores is an important factor which should be dealt with in order to achieve an overall combined better performance on host (SandyBridge) and coprocessors (KNC-MIC).

Acknowledgement. Authors would like to thank Intel IPCC grant and the European Human Brain Project for providing partial funding for this work.

References

1. Carnevale, T., Hines, M.: The NEURON Book. Cambridge University Press, Cambridge (2006)
2. https://www.neuron.yale.edu/neuron/
3. http://www.braininitiative.org/
4. https://www.humanbrainproject.eu/en/
5. Ippen, T., Eppler, J.M., Plesser, H.E., Diesmann, M.: Constructing neuronal network models in massively parallel environments. Front. Neuroinform. **11** (2017). https://doi.org/10.3389/fninf.2017.00030
6. Hines, M., Kumar, S., Schurmann, F.: Comparison of neuronal spike exchange methods on Blue Gene/P supercomputer. Front. Comput. Neurosci. **5**, 49 (2011)
7. Ananthanarayanan, R., Esser, S.K., Simon, H.D., Modha, D.S.: The cat is out of the bag: cortical simulations with 109 neurons and 1013 synapses. In: Supercomputing 09: Proceedings of the ACM/IEEE SC 2009 Conference on High Performance Networking and Computing, Portland, OR (2009). https://doi.org/10.1145/1654059.1654124
8. https://portal.tacc.utexas.edu/archives/stampede/knc
9. https://senselab.med.yale.edu/ModelDB/showmodel.cshtml?model=136803
10. http://www.sdsc.edu/support/user_guides/comet.html
11. http://www.cs.uoregon.edu/research/tau/home.php
12. https://vampir.eu/

Overcoming MPI Communication Overhead for Distributed Community Detection

Naw Safrin Sattar$^{(\boxtimes)}$ and Shaikh Arifuzzaman$^{(\boxtimes)}$

Department of Computer Science, University of New Orleans,
New Orleans, LA 70148, USA
{nsattar,smarifuz}@uno.edu

Abstract. Community detection is an important graph (network) analysis kernel used for discovering functional units and organization of a graph. Louvain method is an efficient algorithm for discovering communities. However, sequential Louvain method does not scale to the emerging large-scale network data. Parallel algorithms designed for modern high performance computing platforms are necessary to process such network big data. Although there are several shared memory based parallel algorithms for Louvain method, those do not scale to a large number of cores and to large networks. One existing Message Passing Interface (MPI) based distributed memory parallel implementation of Louvain algorithm has shown scalability to only 16 processors. In this work, first, we design a shared memory based algorithm using Open MultiProcessing (OpenMP), which shows a 4-fold speedup but is only limited to the physical cores available to our system. Our second algorithm is an MPI-based distributed memory parallel algorithm that scales to a moderate number of processors. We then implement a hybrid algorithm combining the merits from both shared and distributed memory-based approaches. Finally, we incorporate a parallel load balancing scheme, which leads to our final algorithm DPLAL (Distributed Parallel Louvain Algorithm with Load-balancing). DPLAL overcomes the performance bottleneck of the previous algorithms with improved load balancing. We present a comparative analysis of these parallel implementations of Louvain methods using several large real-world networks. DPLAL shows around 12-fold speedup and scales to a larger number of processors.

Keywords: Community detection · Louvain method ·
Parallel algorithms · MPI · OpenMP · Load balancing · Graph mining

1 Introduction

Parallel computing plays a crucial role in processing large-scale graph data [1,2,5,27]. The problem of community detection in graph data arises in many scientific domains [11], e.g., sociology, biology, online media, and transportation.

© Springer Nature Singapore Pte Ltd. 2019
A. Majumdar and R. Arora (Eds.): SCEC 2018, CCIS 964, pp. 77–90, 2019.
https://doi.org/10.1007/978-981-13-7729-7_6

Due to the advancement of data and computing technologies, graph data is growing at an enormous rate. For example, the number of links in social networks [14,26] is growing every millisecond. Processing such graph big data requires the development of parallel algorithms [1–5]. Existing parallel algorithms are developed for both shared memory and distributed memory based systems. Each method has its own merits and demerits. Shared memory based systems are usually limited by the moderate number of available cores [18]. The increase in physical cores is restricted by the scalability of chip sizes. On the other hand, a large number of processing nodes can be used in distributed-memory systems. Although distributed memory based parallelism has the freedom of communicating among processing nodes through passing messages, an efficient communication scheme is required to overcome communication overhead. We present a comparative analysis of our shared and distributed memory based parallel Louvain algorithms, their merits and demerits. We also develop a hybrid parallel Louvain algorithm using the advantage of both shared and distributed memory based approaches. The hybrid algorithm gives us the scope to balance between both shared and distributed memory settings depending on available resources. Load balancing is crucial in parallel computing. A straight-forward distribution with an equal number of vertices per processor might not scale well [2]. We also find that load imbalance also contribute to a higher communication overhead for distributed memory algorithms [4]. A dynamic load balancing [3,25] approach can reduce the idle times of processors leading to increased speedup. Finding a suitable load balancing technique is a challenge in itself as it largely depends on the internal properties of a network and the applications [21]. We present DPLAL, an efficient algorithm for distributed memory setting based on a parallel load balancing scheme and graph partitioning.

2   Related Work

There exists a rich literature of community detection algorithms [6–8,15,16,20, 24,27]. Louvain method [7] is found to be one of the most efficient sequential algorithms [15,16]. In recent years, several works have been done for paralleling Louvain algorithm and a majority of those are shared memory based implementations. These implementations demonstrate only a moderate scalability. One of the fastest shared memory implementations is Grappolo software package [12,17], which is able to process a network with 65.6M vertices using 20 compute cores. One of the MPI based parallel implementations [27] of Louvain method reported scaling for only 16 processors. Later, in [10] the authors could run large graphs with 1,000 processing cores for their MPI implementation but did not provide a comprehensive speedup results. Their MPI+OpenMP implementation demonstrated about 7-fold speedup on 4,000 processors. But the paper uses a higher threshold in lower levels in Louvain method to terminate the level earlier and thus minimized the time contributing to their higher speedup. The work also lacks on the emphasis on graph partitioning and balancing load among the processors. This is a clear contrast with our work where we focused on load balancing issue among others. Our work achieves comparable (or better in many cases) speedups using a significantly fewer number of processors than the work in [10].

3   Background

In this section, we present the Louvain algorithm in brief and discuss the computational model of our parallel algorithms. Note that we use the words *vertex* and *node* interchangeably in the subsequent discussions of this paper. The same is the case for the words *graph* and *network*.

3.1   Louvain Algorithm

Louvain algorithm [7] detects community based on modularity optimization. It demonstrates better performance than other community detection algorithms in terms of computation time and quality of the detected communities [15]. Modularity is calculated using Eq. 1.

$$Q = \frac{1}{2m} \sum_{ij} \left[A_{ij} - \frac{k_i k_j}{2m} \right] \delta\left(c_i c_j\right) \tag{1}$$

Here,

Q = Modularity

A_{ij} = Link weight between nodes i and j

m = Total link weight in the network

k_i = Sum of the link weights attached to node i

c_i = Community to which node i is assigned

$\delta\left(c_i,\ c_j\right)$ = Kronecker delta Value is 1 when nodes i and j are assigned to the same community. Otherwise, the value is 0.

Louvain algorithm has 2 Phases:

- **Modularity Optimization:** This step looks for "small" communities by local optimization of modularity.
- **Community Aggregation:** This step aggregates nodes of the same community to form a super-node and thus create a new smaller network to work on in the next iteration.

Details on the above steps can be found in [7].

3.2   Computational Model

We develop our shared memory based parallel algorithm using Open Multi-Processing (OpenMP) library. Then, we develop our distributed memory based parallel algorithm using Message Passing Interface (MPI). Both MPI and OpenMP have been inscribed in our Hybrid Algorithm. At last, in DPLAL, along with MPI, we use the graph-partitioner METIS [13] to improve graph partitioning and load balancing.

4   Methodology

We present our parallel Louvain algorithms below. Note that we omitted some of the details of these algorithms for brevity. The pseudocode and functional description of our earlier implementation of shared and distributed memory algorithms can be found in [22].

4.1   Shared Memory Parallel Louvain Algorithm

In shared memory based algorithms, there is a shared address space and multiple threads share this common address space. This shared address space can be used efficiently using lock and other synchronization techniques. The main hindrance behind the shared memory based systems is the limited number of processing cores. We parallelize the Louvain algorithm by distributing the computational task among multiple threads using Open Multi-Processing (OpenMP) framework. (See a detailed description of this algorithm in [22].)

4.2   Distributed Memory Parallel Louvain Algorithm

Distributed memory based algorithms can exploit the power of large computing clusters that are widely available now-a-days. The compute nodes have different memory space. Processors exchange messages among themselves to share information. Such inter-processor communication introduces significant overhead, which needs to be minimized. Another crucial challenge is balancing load among processors. We use Message Passing Interface (MPI) for the implementation of distributed memory based parallel Louvain algorithm. In the first phase, we partition the entire network among the processors. Each processor gets a part of the network. In the second phase, each processor complete its computation independently and does communication with other processors whenever necessary. A particular processor is designated as the root or master. After each level of iteration, all processors communicate with the root processor to compute the modularity value of the full network. A detailed functional description of this approach can be found in [22].

4.3   Hybrid Parallel Louvain Algorithm

We use both MPI and OpenMP together to implement the Hybrid Parallel Louvain Algorithm. The hybrid version gives us the flexibility to balance between both shared and distributed memory system. We can tune between shared and distributed memory depending on available resources. In the multi-threading environment, a single thread works for communication among processors and other threads do the computation.

4.4 Distributed Parallel Louvain Algorithm with Load-Balancing

To implement DPLAL, we use the similar approach as described in Sect. 4.2. In the first phase, we have used well-known graph-partitioner METIS [19] to partition our input graph to distribute among the processors. Depending on METIS output, we adjust the number of processors because METIS does not always create same number of partitions as provided in input. We use both edge-cut and communication volume minimization approaches. An empirical comparison of these approaches is described later in Sect. 6. After partitioning, we distribute the input graph among the processors. For second phase, we follow the same flow as described in the Algorithm in [22]. But we have to recompute each function that has been calculated from input graph. Runtime analysis for each of these functions being used in MPI communication has been demonstrated in Sect. 6. Our incorporation of graph partitioning scheme helps minimize the communication overhead of MPI to a great extent and we get an optimized performance from DPLAL.

5 Experimental Setup and Dataset

We describe our experimental setup and datasets below. We use large-scale compute cluster for working on large real-world graph datasets.

5.1 Execution Environment

We use Louisiana Optical Network Infrastructure (LONI) QB2 [9] compute cluster to perform all the experiments. QB2 is a 1.5 Petaflop peak performance cluster containing 504 compute nodes with over 10,000 Intel Xeon processing cores of 2.8 GHz. We use at most 50 computing nodes with 1000 processors for our experiments.

5.2 Description of Datasets

We have used real-world networks from SNAP [23] depicted in Table 1. We have performed our experimentation on different types of network including social networks, internet, peer-to-peer networks, road networks, network with ground truth communities, and Wikipedia networks. All these networks show different structural and organizational properties. This gives us an opportunity to assess the performance of our algorithms for worst case inputs as well. The size of graphs used in our experiments ranges from several hundred thousands to millions of edges.

6 Results

We present the scalability and runtime analysis of our algorithms below. We discuss the trade-offs and challenges alongside.

Table 1. Datasets used in our experimental evaluation.

Network	Vertices	Edges	Description
email-Eu-core	1,005	25,571	Email network from a large European research institution
ego-Facebook	4,039	88,234	Social circles ('friends lists') from Facebook
wiki-Vote	7,115	103,689	Wikipedia who-votes-on-whom network
p2p-Gnutella08	6,301	20,777	A sequence of snapshots of the Gnutella peer-to-peer file sharing network for different dates of August 2002
p2p-Gnutella09	8,114	26,013	
p2p-Gnutella04	10,876	39,994	
p2p-Gnutella25	22,687	54,705	
p2p-Gnutella30	36,682	88,328	
p2p-Gnutella31	62,586	147,892	
soc-Slashdot0922	82,168	948,464	Slashdot social network from February 2009
com-DBLP	317,080	1,049,866	DBLP collaboration (co-authorship) network
roadNet-PA	1,088,092	1,541,898	Pennsylvania road network

Speedup Factors of Shared and Distributed Memory Algorithms. We design both shared and distributed memory based algorithms for Louvain methods. The speedup results are shown in Fig. 1a and b. Our shared memory and distributed memory based algorithms achieve speedups of around 4 and 1.5, respectively. The number of physical processing core available to our system is 20. Our shared memory algorithm scales well to this many cores. However, due to the unavailability of large shared memory system, we also design distributed memory algorithm. Further, shared memory algorithms show a limited scalability to large networks as discussed in [6]. Our distributed memory algorithm demonstrates only a minimal speedup for 30 processors. The inter-processor communication severely affects the speedup of this algorithm. We strive to overcome such communication bottleneck by designing hybrid algorithm.

Speedup Factors of Our Hybrid Parallel Algorithm. Our hybrid algorithm tends to find a balance between the above two approaches, shared and distributed memory. As shown in Fig. 1c, we get a speedup of around 2 for the hybrid implementation of Louvain algorithm. The speedup is similar to the MPI implementation. It is evident that in multi-threading environment runtime will decrease as workload is distributed among the threads. But we observe that in some cases, both single and multiple threads take similar time. Even sometimes multiple threads take more time than a single thread. It indicates that hybrid implementation also suffers from the communication overhead problem

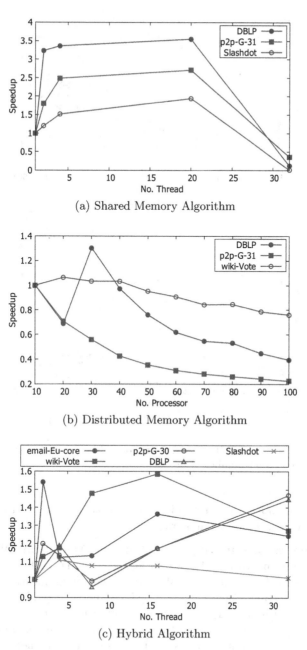

(a) Shared Memory Algorithm

(b) Distributed Memory Algorithm

(c) Hybrid Algorithm

Fig. 1. Speedup factors of our parallel Louvain algorithms for different types of networks. Our hybrid algorithm strikes a balance between shared and distributed memory based algorithms.

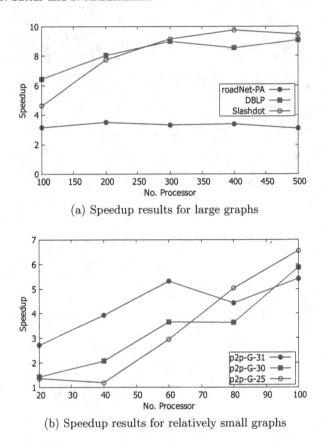

(a) Speedup results for large graphs

(b) Speedup results for relatively small graphs

Fig. 2. Speedup factors of DPLAL algorithm for different types of networks. Larger networks scale to a larger number of processors.

alike MPI. Communication overhead of distributed memory setting limits the performance of hybrid algorithm as well.

Speedup Factors of Our Improved Parallel Algorithm DPLAL. Our final parallel implementation of Louvain algorithm is DPLAL. This algorithm achieves a speedup factor up-to 12. We reduce the communication overhead in message passing setting to a great extent by introducing a load balancing scheme during graph partitioning. The improved speedup for DPLAL is presented in Fig. 2. For larger networks, our algorithm scales to a larger number of processors. We are able to use around a thousand processors. For smaller networks, the algorithm scales to a couple of hundred processors. It is understandable that for smaller networks, the communication overhead gradually offsets the advantage obtained from parallel computation. However, since we want to use a larger number of processors to work on larger networks, our algorithm in fact has this desirable property. Overall, DPLAL algorithm scales well with the increase in the number of processors and to large networks.

Runtime Analysis: A Breakdown of Execution Times. We present a breakdown of executions times. Figure 3 shows the runtime analysis for our largest network RoadNet-PA. We observe that communication time for *gathering neighbor information* and *exchanging duality resolved community* decreases with increasing number of processors. Communication time for both *exchanging updated community* and *gathering updated community* increases up-to a certain number of processors and after decreasing, the time becomes almost constant. Among all these communications, time to gather communities at the root processor takes maximum time and contribute to the high runtime.

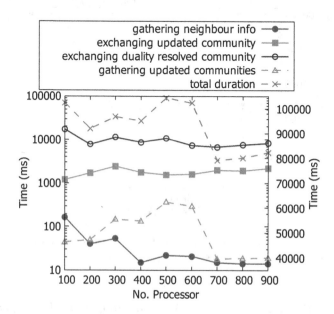

Fig. 3. Runtime analysis of RoadNet-PA graph with DPLAL algorithm for varied number of processors. We show a breakdown of execution times for different modules or functions in the algorithm. Time for *gathering updated communities* and *total duration* are plotted w.r.t the right *y*-axis.

Number of Processors Versus Execution Time. For many large networks that we experimented on (including the ones in Fig. 2a), we find that those can scale to up to ≈800 processors. We call this number as the *optimum number of processors* for those networks. This optimum number depends on network size. As our focus is on larger networks, to find out the relationship between runtime and network size, we keep the number of processor 800 fixed and run an experiment. As shown in Fig. 4, the communication time for *gathering neighbor info* decreases with growing network size whereas both time for *gathering updated communities* and *exchanging duality resolved community* increase. Communication time for *exchanging updated community* increases up-to a certain point and then starts decreasing afterwards. For larger networks ($>8K$), total runtime increases proportionately with growing network size. As smaller graphs do not scale to 800 processors, these do not follow the trend, but it can be inferred that these will behave the same way for their optimum number of processors.

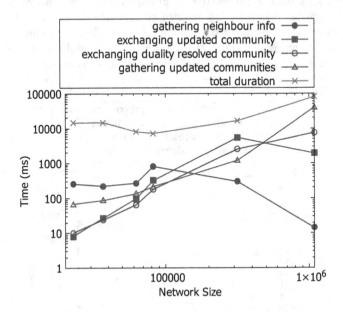

Fig. 4. Increase in runtime of DPLAL algorithm with an increase in the sizes of the graphs keeping the number of processors fixed.

METIS Partitioning Approaches. We also compare the METIS partitioning techniques, between edge-cut and communication volume minimization, to find out the efficient approach for our algorithm. Figure 5 shows the runtime comparison between edge-cut and communication volume minimization techniques. We find that the communication volume minimization approach always takes similar or higher time than that of edge-cut partitioning. So, in our subsequent experimentation, we have used edge-cut partitioning approach.

7   Performance Analysis

We present a comparative analysis of our algorithms, its sequential version, and another existing distributed memory algorithm.

7.1   Comparison with Other Parallel Algorithms

We compare the performance of DPLAL with another distributed memory parallel implementation of Louvain method given in Wickramaarachchi et al. [27].

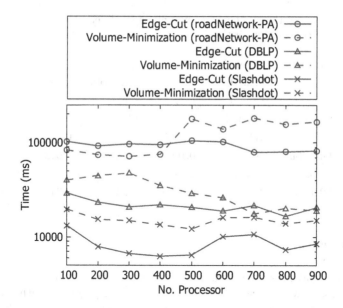

Fig. 5. Comparison of METIS partitioning approaches (edge-cut versus communication volume minimization) for several networks. The edge-cut approach achieves better runtime efficiency for the above real-world networks.

For a network with 500,000 nodes, Wickramaarachchi et al. achieved a maximum speedup of 6 whereas with DPLAL for a network with 317,080 nodes we get a speedup of 12 using 800 processors. The largest network processed by them has 8M nodes and achieved a speedup of 4. Our largest network achieves a comparable speedup (4-fold speedup with 1M nodes). The work in [27] did not report runtime results so we could not compare our runtime with theirs directly. Their work reported scalability to only 16 processors whereas our algorithm is able to scale to almost a thousand of processors.

7.2   Comparison with Sequential Algorithm

We have compared our algorithms with the sequential version [7] to analyze the accuracy of our implementations. Deviation of the number of communities between sequential and our implementations is represented in Table 2. The deviation is negligible compared to network size. The number of communities is not constant and they vary because of the randomization introduced in the Louvain algorithm. Table 2 gives an approximation of the communities.

Although shared memory based parallel Louvain has the least deviation, the speedup is not remarkable. Whereas, DPLAL shows a moderate deviation but its speedup is 3 times of that of shared parallel Louvain algorithm.

Table 2. Deviation of the number of communities for different parallel Louvain Algorithms from the sequential algorithm.

| Algorithm | Network | | | |
| | com-DBLP | | wiki-Vote | |
	Comm. No.	Dev. (%)	Comm. No.	Dev. (%)
Sequential	109,104	–	1,213	–
Shared	109,102	.0006	1,213	0
Distributed	109,441	0.106	1,216	0.042
Hybrid	104,668	1.39	1,163	0.71
DPLAL	109,063	0.0129	1,210	0.042

8   Conclusion

Our parallel algorithms for Louvain method demonstrate good speedup on several types of real-world graphs. As instance, for DBLP graph with 0.3 million nodes, we get speedups of around 4, 1.5 and 2 for shared memory, distributed memory, and hybrid implementations, respectively. Among these three algorithms, shared memory parallel algorithm gives better speedup than others. However, shared memory system has limited number of physical cores and might not be able to process very large networks. A large network often requires distributed processing and each computing node stores and works with a part of the entire network. As we plan to work with networks with billions of nodes and edges, we work towards the improvement of the scalability of our algorithms by reducing the communication overhead. We have identified the problems for each implementation and come up with an optimized implementation **DPLAL**. With our improved algorithm DPLAL, community detection in DBLP network achieves a 12-fold speedup. Our largest network, roadNetwork-PA has 4-fold speedup for same number of processors. With increasing network size, number of processor also increases. We will work with larger networks increasing the number of processors in our future work. The optimum number of processor largely depends on the network size. We will also experiment with other load-balancing schemes to find an efficient load balancing scheme to make DPLAL more scalable. We also want to eliminate the effect of small communities that create misconception to understand the community structure and its properties. Further, we will explore the effect of node ordering (e.g., degree based ordering, random ordering) on the performance of parallel Louvain algorithms.

Acknowledgements. This work has been partially supported by Louisiana Board of Regents RCS Grant LEQSF(2017-20)-RDA- 25 and University of New Orleans ORSP Award CON000000002410. We also thank the anonymous reviewers for the helpful comments and suggestions to improve this paper.

References

1. Arifuzzaman, S., Khan, M.: Fast parallel conversion of edge list to adjacency list for large-scale graphs. In: 2015 Proceedings of the 23rd Symposium on High Performance Computing, pp. 17–24. Society for Computer Simulation International (2015)
2. Arifuzzaman, S., Khan, M., Marathe, M.: PATRIC: a parallel algorithm for counting triangles in massive networks. In: Proceedings of the 22nd ACM International Conference on Information & Knowledge Management, pp. 529–538. ACM (2013)
3. Arifuzzaman, S., Khan, M., Marathe, M.: A fast parallel algorithm for counting triangles in graphs using dynamic load balancing. In: 2015 IEEE International Conference on Big Data (Big Data), pp. 1839–1847. IEEE (2015)
4. Arifuzzaman, S., Khan, M., Marathe, M.: A space-efficient parallel algorithm for counting exact triangles in massive networks. In: 2015 IEEE 17th International Conference on High Performance Computing and Communications (HPCC), pp. 527–534. IEEE (2015)
5. Arifuzzaman, S., Pandey, B.: Scalable mining and analysis of protein-protein interaction networks. In: 3rd International Conference on Big Data Intelligence and Computing (DataCom 2017), pp. 1098–1105. IEEE (2017)
6. Bhowmick, S., Srinivasan, S.: A template for parallelizing the Louvain method for modularity maximization. In: Mukherjee, A., Choudhury, M., Peruani, F., Ganguly, N., Mitra, B. (eds.) Dynamics on and of Complex Networks, vol. 2, pp. 111–124. Springer, New York (2013). https://doi.org/10.1007/978-1-4614-6729-8_6
7. Blondel, V.D., Guillaume, J.L., Lambiotte, R., Lefebvre, E.: Fast unfolding of communities in large networks. J. Stat. Mech.: Theory Exp. **2008**(10), P10008 (2008)
8. Clauset, A., Newman, M.E., Moore, C.: Finding community structure in very large networks. Phys. Rev. E **70**(6), 066111 (2004)
9. Documentation—user guides—qb2. http://www.hpc.lsu.edu/docs/guides.php?system=QB2
10. Ghosh, S., et al.: Distributed Louvain algorithm for graph community detection. In: 2018 IEEE International Parallel and Distributed Processing Symposium (IPDPS), pp. 885–895. IEEE (2018)
11. Girvan, M., Newman, M.E.: Community structure in social and biological networks. Proc. Nat. Acad. Sci. **99**(12), 7821–7826 (2002)
12. Halappanavar, M., Lu, H., Kalyanaraman, A., Tumeo, A.: Scalable static and dynamic community detection using Grappolo. In: 2017 IEEE High Performance Extreme Computing Conference (HPEC), pp. 1–6. IEEE (2017)
13. Karypis, G., Kumar, V.: A fast and high quality multilevel scheme for partitioning irregular graphs. SIAM J. Sci. Comput. **20**(1), 359–392 (1998)
14. Kwak, H., Lee, C., Park, H., Moon, S.: What is twitter, a social network or a news media? In: Proceedings of the 19th International Conference on World Wide Web, pp. 591–600. ACM (2010)
15. Lancichinetti, A., Fortunato, S.: Community detection algorithms: a comparative analysis. Phys. Rev. E **80**(5), 056117 (2009)

16. Leskovec, J., Lang, K.J., Mahoney, M.: Empirical comparison of algorithms for network community detection. In: Proceedings of the 19th International Conference on World Wide Web, pp. 631–640. ACM (2010)
17. Lu, H., Halappanavar, M., Kalyanaraman, A.: Parallel heuristics for scalable community detection. Parallel Comput. **47**, 19–37 (2015)
18. McCalpin, J.D., et al.: Memory bandwidth and machine balance in current high performance computers. In: 1995 IEEE Computer Society Technical Committee on Computer Architecture (TCCA) Newsletter, pp. 19–25 (1995)
19. Karypis Lab: METIS - serial graph partitioning and fill-reducing matrix ordering. http://glaros.dtc.umn.edu/gkhome/metis/metis/overview
20. Raghavan, U.N., Albert, R., Kumara, S.: Near linear time algorithm to detect community structures in large-scale networks. Phys. Rev. E **76**(3), 036106 (2007)
21. Raval, A., Nasre, R., Kumar, V., Vadhiyar, S., Pingali, K., et al.: Dynamic load balancing strategies for graph applications on GPUs. arXiv preprint arXiv:1711.00231 (2017)
22. Sattar, N., Arifuzzaman, S.: Parallelizing Louvain algorithm: distributed memory challenges. In: 2018 IEEE 16th International Conference on Dependable, Autonomic and Secure Computing (DASC 2018), pp. 695–701. IEEE (2018)
23. Stanford large network dataset collection. https://snap.stanford.edu/data/index.html
24. Staudt, C.L., Meyerhenke, H.: Engineering parallel algorithms for community detection in massive networks. IEEE Trans. Parallel Distrib. Syst. **27**(1), 171–184 (2016)
25. Talukder, N., Zaki, M.J.: Parallel graph mining with dynamic load balancing. In: 2016 IEEE International Conference on Big Data (Big Data), pp. 3352–3359. IEEE (2016)
26. Ugander, J., Karrer, B., Backstrom, L., Marlow, C.: The anatomy of the Facebook social graph. arXiv preprint arXiv:1111.4503 (2011)
27. Wickramaarachchi, C., Frincuy, M., Small, P., Prasannay, V.: Fast parallel algorithm for unfolding of communities in large graphs. In: 2014 IEEE High Performance Extreme Computing Conference (HPEC), pp. 1–6. IEEE (2014)

Analyzing IO Usage Patterns of User Jobs to Improve Overall HPC System Efficiency

Syed Sadat Nazrul, Cherie Huang, Mahidhar Tatineni, Nicole Wolter,
Dmitry Mishin, Trevor Cooper, and Amit Majumdar[✉]

San Diego Supercomputer Center, University of California San Diego,
La Jolla, CA 92093, USA
majumdar@sdsc.edu

Abstract. This work looks at analyzing I/O traffic of users' jobs on a HPC machine for a period of time. Monitoring tools are collecting the data in a continuous basis on the HPC system. We looked at aggregate I/O data usage patterns of users' jobs on the system both on the parallel shared Lustre file system and the node-local SSDs. Data mining tools are then applied to analyze the I/O usage pattern data in an attempt to tie the data to particular codes that produced those I/O behaviors from users' jobs.

Keywords: Aggregate I/O usage data · Data mining · Application I/O behavior

1 Introduction

Efficient utilization of large scale High Performance Computing (HPC) systems is extremely important from both system utilization point of view and data center operation point of view. Many HPC systems today have special software that is used to continuously collect all kinds of information related to users' jobs such as interconnect traffic, file system traffic, CPU utilization, etc. This data needs to be analyzed to see what information can be extracted about users' jobs and if that information can be used to improve a HPC system operation. While some data is used to monitor the system status, it also can be analyzed to provide deeper insight into potential patterns of system component utilization by users. This knowledge can then be applied to future configuration changes such as more optimized scheduling which can benefit both the users and the systems, and even for architecting future HPC machines. For example, is it possible to identify class of user jobs which do heavy I/O versus which do not and then schedule them optimally?

Given the plethora of data, the real question is how to analyze large amounts of HPC systems data in such a way that patterns can be identified and deeply examined. While the possibilities of analyzing the data are endless, our project focuses on analyzing file system I/O traffic of users jobs. We are employing data mining methods and machine learning algorithms as analyzation tools. We discuss the steps of data collection, data processing, and data analysis involved in the study of such data produced from the Comet supercomputer at the San Diego Supercomputer Center (SDSC), University of California San Diego.

A. Majumdar and R. Arora (Eds.): SCEC 2018, CCIS 964, pp. 91–102, 2019.
https://doi.org/10.1007/978-981-13-7729-7_7

2   Comet and Data Collection

Since May 2015, the National Science Foundation funded Comet HPC system housed at SDSC, has been in production for the national user community [1]. This HPC system is a Dell cluster delivering ~2.0 petaflops of Compute power. It consists of Intel Haswell processors, along with AVX2 and Mellanox FDR Infiniband networks. Comet's standard Compute nodes are built with Intel Xeon E5-2680v3 (formerly codenamed Haswell) processors, 128 GB DDR4 Dram (64 GB per socket), and 320 GB of SSD local scratch memory. Comet also has GPU nodes (K80 and P100) which have four NVIDIA GPUs each. Comet's large memory nodes each contain 1.5 TB of DRAM and four Haswell processors. The network topology is 56 Gbps FDR InfiniBand with rack-level full bisection bandwidth and 4:1 oversubscription cross-rack bandwidth. Comet has 7 petabytes of 200 GB/s performance storage and 6 petabytes of 100 GB/s durable storage. NFS is used primarily for home directory of Comet's users. This HPC system is currently serving many hundreds of academic users from various universities in the US, and the user jobs are related to simulations from a wide variety of science, engineering and social science disciplines. It allows users to choose from three separate queues, with each queue mapping to a specific node type the users would like their jobs to run on. The Compute Queue allows users to run exclusively on Comet's standard Compute nodes, while the GPU Queue allows users to run on Comet GPU nodes. Users can also choose the Shared Queue in which users run jobs in shared mode on Comet shared nodes. The scheduling for the three queues is implemented by SLURM (Simple Linux Utility for Resource Management).

Since Comet became available in mid-2015, the TACC Stats [2] software has been collecting and monitoring all kinds of users' job related data on the system. The way it is set up on Comet, it collects user job's I/O stats on file systems every 10 min interval. This data includes information about roughly 700,000 jobs (from Compute Queue and GPU Queue) that ran during the June 2015 to November 2015 time period, and is around 500 GB in size. Currently this information is still growing in size as TACC Stats is continuously collecting data as more and more jobs are run through the system.

3   Data Processing and Storage

In order to more efficiently analyze the data, I/O related measurements as well as basic job metadata were extracted into a custom database like structure. This was done from the pickle file data where TACC Stats collected data is stored. Figure 1 shows the data processing flowchart. The pickle database isolates file system I/O performance and characteristics of these 700,000 user jobs into NFS I/O, the Lustre parallel file system I/O, and the node local SSD I/O. In order to better understand potential interconnect traffic interference due to switch level edge cases, Infiniband information is also stored in the database. In the interest of making sure the analysis results were not skewed by multiple job interference, the I/O data was only taken from the Compute Queue and the GPU Queue jobs. Shared queue jobs were left out for the first pass analysis. The I/O data are stored in ways that can be quickly extracted as inputs for machine learning algorithms and also allow for generation of easy visualization of I/O performance of each user's job.

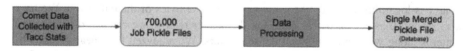

Fig. 1. A flowchart of raw data to custom pickle database.

The IOR benchmark [3] was run to test the pipeline since we can control the IO that is generated by the IOR benchmark. IOR benchmarks for Lustre I/O, SSD I/O, and NFS I/O were done and the TACC Stats results were extracted from the pickle files and plotted to verify the functionality of the flowchart. The plot in Fig. 2 verified that expected IOR SSD IO results were truly picked up by the process. In the plot 'block: wr_sectors' is SSD write I/O. The value is represented in bytes.

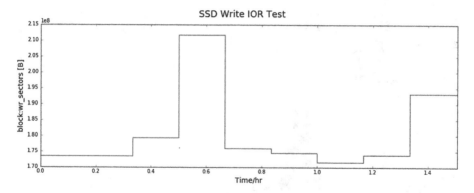

Fig. 2. Sample IOR benchmark.

4 Data Analysis

Blind exploration of statistical data and plots were the first step of the analysis stage before utilizing supervised and unsupervised learning approaches. This understanding was used to more specifically narrow down the I/O reads and writes for Lustre, SSDs, and the NFS. Python's Scikit-learn [5] machine learning library and its Principal Component Analysis (PCA) algorithm were used for dimensionality reduction in the interest of reducing noise. The data were then clustered using unsupervised learning methods and algorithms like Density-Based Spatial Clustering of Applications with Noise (DBSCAN) [4] and Scikit Learn implementation of k-Means [5]. The clustering of the jobs has allowed some insightful observations on similar I/O behavior among bunch of jobs, and how different groups of jobs might be showing different I/O behavior.

4.1   Scatter Matrix

In order to have a better idea of our dataset, we visualize all the Compute Queue and GPU Queue jobs' I/O on a scatter matrix from Scikit-learn [5] and set the alpha value to 2 for better visualization as shown in Fig. 3. For each user job the scale of the scatter matrix is logarithm of base 10 for the aggregate I/O bytes of the entire job. We have also set log 0 as −2 on our scaling. On the scatter matrix, we can see distinct linear patterns along with spots of small dense clusters. We analyzed the linear patterns by looking at the job names and project names of the jobs that fall within those lines. This allowed us to estimate the possible applications of the jobs that are forming those patterns. For the spots, it is too difficult for us to manually look at all the spots individually. Hence, we decided to use clustering algorithms for unsupervised learning. The clustering algorithms used were k-Means and DBSCAN.

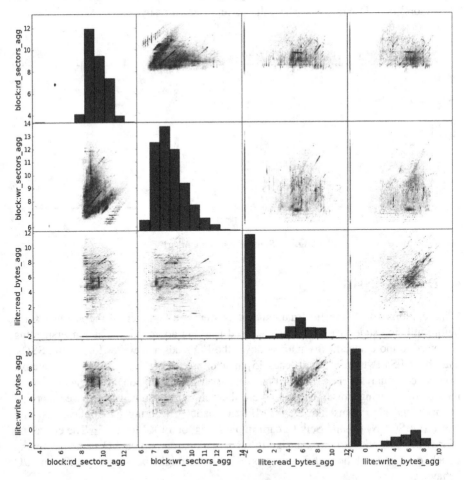

Fig. 3. Scatter matrix (llite refers to Lustre; block refers to SSD).

Linear Pattern

From our scatter matrix, we have analyzed the jobs in each linear pattern and have explained the significant ones below. For each linear pattern the jobs we analyzed are bounded by the purple lines in the figures below. Each pattern will have a RAW image that shows the scatter plot on its own and the TARGET image that highlights the jobs of the pattern of interest.

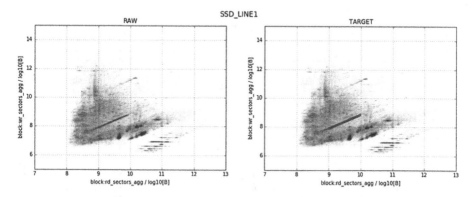

Fig. 4. Block read versus block write pattern (SSD_LINE1) – lower line.

SSD_LINE1 (Fig. 4) is one of the linear patterns formed when analyzing aggregate write I/O and aggregate read I/O on the SSD. Pertaining to all the jobs that are part of this pattern, we have seen that 1,877 (76%) jobs are Phylogentics Gateway (called CIPRES running RXML code) and Neuroscience Gateway (running spiking neuronal simulation) jobs. We know that these jobs only produce I/O to NFS. However they used OpenMPI for their MPI communication. This leads to runtime I/O activity (for example memory map information) in/tmp which is located on the SSDs.

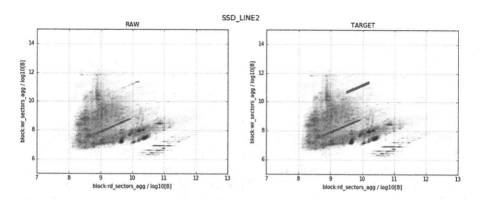

Fig. 5. Block read versus block write pattern (SSD_LINE2) – upper line.

SSD_LINE2 (Fig. 5) is another linear pattern formed when analyzing aggregate write I/O and aggregate read I/O on the SSD. Pertaining to all the jobs that are part of this pattern, we have seen that 208 (82%) jobs have the same job name and from a particular project group. Further investigation and discussion with the user showed that these I/O patterns were produced by Hadoop jobs. On Comet, Hadoop is configured to use local scratch (SSD) as the basis for its HDFS file system. Hence, as expected, there is a significant amount of I/O to SSDs from these jobs.

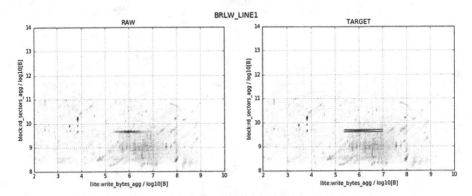

Fig. 6. Block read versus lustre write pattern (BRLW_LINE1).

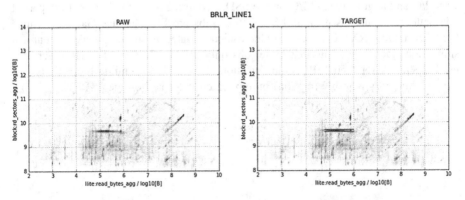

Fig. 7. Block read versus lustre read pattern (BRLR_LINE1) – horizontal line.

BRLW_LINE1 (Fig. 6) and BRLR_LINE1 (Fig. 7) are horizontal linear patterns on SSD read I/O against Lustre Write I/O and Lustre Read I/O respectively. They both show similar patterns. This indicates that they were both created by similar applications. BRLW_LINE1 contains 232 (28%) VASP and CP2 K jobs and 134 (16%) NAMD jobs. Hence, we can say these applications require ∼4 GB of read from the local SSD (this includes both scratch and system directories) and between 100 kB and 10 MB Lustre I/O (both read and write) to run the job.

Spots of Small Dense Clusters

After analyzing the linear patterns, we will analyze the spots of small dense clusters using clustering algorithms for unsupervised learning. For our purpose, we will be using k-Means and DBSCAN.

K-means Clustering

k-Means clustering is a method of vector quantization, originally from signal processing, that is popular for cluster analysis in data mining. k-Means clustering aims to partition n observations into k clusters in which each observation belongs to the cluster with the nearest mean, serving as a prototype of the cluster. This results in a partitioning of the data space into Voronoi cells. k-Means is carried out using the Scikit-Learn implementation [5]. The k-Means algorithm was performed on aggregate I/O data.

For estimating the cluster centers by minimizing the sum of square distance of each point from the cluster center. If the sum of the square distance was less than 0.0001, we assumed that the number of cluster to be optimal. This method showed that the optimal number of clusters is 13.

The k-Means clustering produced the clusters (along with the cluster ID, percentage composition of jobs and percentage composition of unique users) shown in Table 1.

Table 1. k-Means clusters.

ID	Jobs	Users
0	235195 (97.09%)	838 (99.64%)
1	1 (0.00%)	1 (0.12%)
2	220 (0.09%)	8 (0.95%)
3	37 (0.02%)	6 (0.71%)
s4	283 (0.12%)	58 (6.90%)
5	933 (0.39%)	145 (17.24%)
s6	4 (0.00%)	3 (0.36%)
7	20 (0.01%)	3 (0.36%)
8	26 (0.01%)	4 (0.48%)
9	1 (0.00%)	1 (0.12%)
10	340 (0.14%)	16 (1.90%)
11	5045 (2.08%)	357 (42.45%)
12	144 (0.06%)	18 (2.14%)

We have also taken the k-Means analysis and applied it to our scatter matrix, along with the cluster centers as 'X' on Fig. 8. Among all the clusters, one of the clusters of interest was cluster 10. The teal colored cluster (number 10 in Table 1), as shown in Fig. 8, is characterized by low SSD read and SSD write (100 MB–1 GB). However, this cluster shows very high Lustre read (>10 GB) and variable Lustre write (100 kB–1 GB). At least 324 (89%) of these jobs had projects that indicate that these are astrophysics jobs.

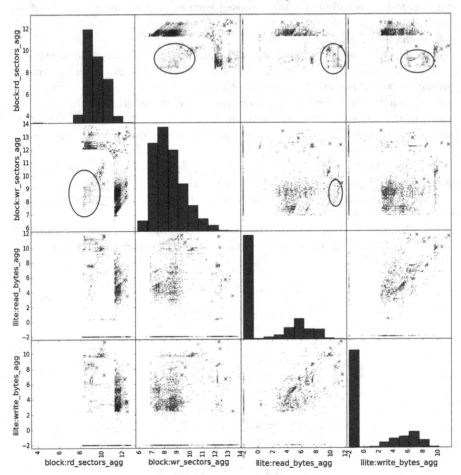

Fig. 8. K-Means analysis (cluster center marks 'X' and cluster 10 encircled). (Color figure online)

DBSCAN Clustering

Density-based spatial clustering of applications with noise (DBSCAN) is a data clustering algorithm proposed by Ester, Kriegel, Sander and Xu in 1996 [4]. It is a density-based clustering algorithm: given a set of points in some space, it groups together points that are closely packed together (points with many nearby neighbors), marking as outliers points that lie alone in low-density regions (whose nearest neighbors are too far away). DBSCAN is one of the most common clustering algorithms and also most cited in scientific literature. In 2014, the algorithm was awarded the test of time award (an award given to algorithms which have received substantial attention in theory and practice) at the leading data mining conference, KDD.

A custom made DBSCAN algorithm, which was accelerated by multiplexing different similarity queries. [6] The DBSCAN algorithm was performed on aggregate I/O data. For this implementation, we used the DBSCAN parameters of minimum points of 150 and epsilon value of 0.0003. These parameters were picked to get the number of clusters to be the same as k-Means. These combination of parameters produced 14 clusters as shown in Table 2.

Table 2. DBSCAN clusters.

ID	Jobs	Users
0	2219 (0.92%)	128 (15.22%)
1	114470 (47.25%)	722 (85.85%)
2	6630 (2.74%)	310 (36.86%)
3	4637 (1.91%)	244 (29.01%)
4	1062 (0.44%)	111 (13.20%)
5	414 (0.17%)	59 (7.02%)
6	352 (0.15%)	95 (11.30%)
7	451 (0.19%)	71 (8.44%)
8	295 (0.12%)	60 (7.13%)
9	277 (0.11%)	50 (5.95%)
10	267 (0.11%)	64 (7.61%)
11	242 (0.10%)	56 (6.66%)
12	159 (0.07%)	27 (3.21%)
−1	110774 (45.73%)	762 (90.61%)

In Table 2, cluster −1 are jobs that could not be categorized in the above clusters. Among all the clusters, as shown in Fig. 9, one of the interesting clusters is number 7. The olive green cluster (number 7 on Table 2), as shown on Fig. 9, shows a distinct quarter ring pattern for SSD read vs SSD write. The SSD I/O usage ranges within 1 to 10 GB. In comparison, the olive green cluster forms a small line on Lustre read vs Lustre write. The Lustre read is relatively constant around 10 B while the Lustre write ranges between 100 kB to 1 MB. 183 (73%) of the jobs on this cluster are from the field of molecular biophysics.

Since 46% of the jobs on our DBSCAN cluster analysis could not be categorized on any identified cluster, we decided to reduce the minimum points parameter of the algorithm. However, the number of clusters and the composition of cluster −1 barely changed when we reduced our minimum points value as low as 50. Hence, we concluded our DBSCAN analysis.

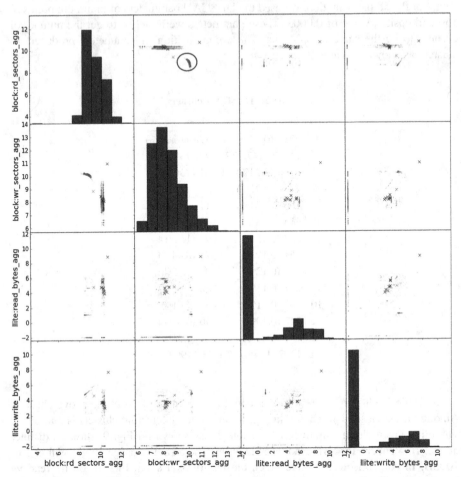

Fig. 9. DBSCAN analysis (cluster center marks 'X' and cluster 7 encircled). (Color figure online)

4.2   Analysis of Longer Jobs

Since we were unable to analyze the time series of a lot of jobs from our identified patterns as most of the jobs ran for less than 10 min, we have decided to perform a scatter matrix analysis of jobs that ran for more than 1 h. This can be seen in Fig. 10. However, we could not derive any reliable pattern from the aggregate I/O data of this particular dataset. For future work, looking into the time series data will be of interest.

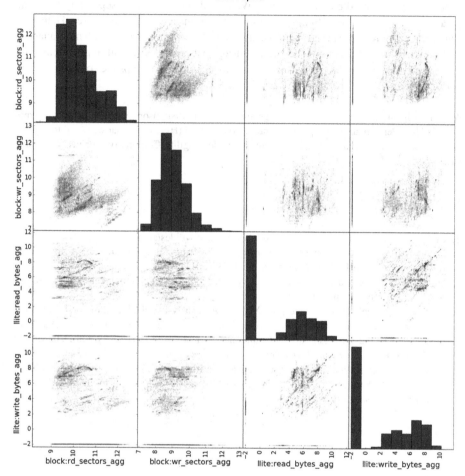

Fig. 10. Scatter matrix of longer jobs.

5 Conclusion

Using aggregate I/O data from jobs that used the SSD and Lustre file systems on San Diego Supercomputer Center's Comet cluster, we were able to analyze distinct patterns in the dataset caused by different applications. We have seen that processes unrelated to NFS based gateway jobs created a distinct linear pattern on the SSD read vs SSD write plot. We were also able to identify distinct patterns generated by astrophysics, molecular dynamics and Hadoop based applications. In this project due to the limited time duration of the project (two months), we were only able to analyze the aggregate I/O for each job although we have time series I/O data available. However, even with this limited information, we were able to identify I/O behaviors of different job applications. In the future, we can further analyze the time series data. For example, we can attempt to break up the time series of the jobs based on I/O usage at the beginning of the job, at the middle and at the end. We can also analyze jobs separately based on parameters like run time of the job, known applications and even edge cases. Hence we can extract different meaningful information based on further analysis. These analysis will allow us to better understand the I/O usage patterns of different applications with the possibility using the information in a scheduler to improve overall system performance.

Acknowledgement. Authors acknowledge funding support/sponsorship from Engility Corporation's High Performance Computing Center of Excellence (HPC CoE) that was used to support the student research. Authors thank Dr. Rajiv Bendale, Engility Corporation, for many valuable suggestions for this project.

References

1. Comet User Guide. http://www.sdsc.edu/support/user_guides/comet.html
2. Hammond, J.: TACC stats: I/O performance monitoring for the instransigent. In: Invited Keynote for the 3rd IASDS Workshop, pp. 1–29 (2011)
3. http://www.nersc.gov/users/computational-systems/cori/nersc-8-procurement/trinity-nersc-8-rfp/nersc-8-trinity-benchmarks/ior/
4. Ester, M., Kriegel, H.-P., Sander, J., Xu, X.: A density-based algorithm for discovering clusters in large spatial databases with noise. In: Simoudis, E., Han, J., Fayyad, U.M. (eds.) Proceedings of the 2nd International Conference on Knowledge Discovery and Data Mining (KDD-1996), pp. 226–231. AAAI Press (1996)
5. Pedregosa, F., et al.: Scikit-learn: machine learning in Python. JMLR **12**, 2825–2830 (2011)
6. Kriegel, H.-P., Kroeger, P., Sander, J., Zimek, A.: Density-based clustering. WIREs Data Min. Knowl. Discov. **1**(3), 231–240 (2011)

Science Gateways

Scalable Software Infrastructure for Integrating Supercomputing with Volunteer Computing and Cloud Computing

Ritu Arora[1(✉)], Carlos Redondo[2], and Gerald Joshua[2]

[1] Texas Advanced Computing Center, University of Texas at Austin, Austin, TX, USA
rauta@tacc.utexas.edu
[2] University of Texas at Austin, Austin, TX, USA
{carlos.red,gerald.joshua153}@utexass.edu

Abstract. Volunteer Computing (VC) is a computing model that uses donated computing cycles on the devices such as laptops, desktops, and tablets to do scientific computing. BOINC is the most popular software framework for VC and it helps in connecting the projects needing computing cycles with the volunteers interested in donating the computing cycles on their resources. It has already enabled projects with high societal impact to harness several PetaFLOPs of donated computing cycles. Given its potential in elastically augmenting the capacity of existing supercomputing resources for running High-Throughput Computing (HTC) jobs, we have extended the BOINC software infrastructure and have made it amenable for integration with the supercomputing and cloud computing environments. We have named the extension of the BOINC software infrastructure as BOINC@TACC, and are using it to route *qualified* HTC jobs from the supercomputers at the Texas Advanced Computing Center (TACC) to not only the typically volunteered devices but also to the cloud computing resources such as Jetstream and Chameleon. BOINC@TACC can be extremely useful for those researchers/scholars who are running low on allocations of compute-cycles on the supercomputers, or are interested in reducing the turnaround time of their HTC jobs when the supercomputers are oversubscribed. We have also developed a web-application for TACC users so that, through the convenience of their web-browser, they can submit their HTC jobs for running on the resources volunteered by the community. An overview of the BOINC@TACC project is presented in this paper. The BOINC@TACC software infrastructure is open-source and can be easily adapted for use by other supercomputing centers that are interested in building their volunteer community and connecting them with the researchers needing multi-petascale (and even exascale) computing power for their HTC jobs.

© Springer Nature Singapore Pte Ltd. 2019
A. Majumdar and R. Arora (Eds.): SCEC 2018, CCIS 964, pp. 105–119, 2019.
https://doi.org/10.1007/978-981-13-7729-7_8

1   Introduction

Due to the constantly increasing need for running large-scale applications, the supercomputing resources at open-science data centers can be over-subscribed at times, and when this happens, the turnaround time of small High-Throughput Computing (HTC) jobs can be longer than expected. To reduce the turnaround time of the small HTC jobs in such situations, these jobs can be routed to external computing resources. Such routing depends upon the users' consent to take advantage of the external resources, and the characteristics of their jobs, such as, the (1) anticipated job completion time, (2) amount of data to be ingested or produced during the job run, (3) amount of memory needed during run-time, and the (4) type of hardware resources needed (i.e., CPU or GPU).

The researchers may also be interested in using the external computing resources when they are running low on the compute-time granted to them through a competitive resource allocation process. Typically, it is hard to get 100% of the requested allocation of compute-time on the supercomputers that are in high-demand. Therefore, users with unsatisfied computational needs have to find additional resources to supplement their allocations. The additional computing resources can be an agglomeration of laptops, desktops, tablets, and the VMs in the cloud, and the computing cycles on these resources can be donated by the volunteers in the community, thereby, making the Volunteer Computing (VC) model relevant to the supercomputing user community.

We formally define VC as a computing model that uses donated computing cycles on devices such as laptops, desktops, and tablets to do scientific computing. BOINC [1] is the most popular software framework for VC and helps in connecting the projects needing computing cycles with the volunteers interested in donating the computing cycles on their resources. It has a client-server architecture, and has already enabled projects with high societal impact to harness several PetaFLOPs of donated computing cycles.

Given its potential in elastically augmenting the capacity of existing supercomputing resources for running HTC jobs, we have extended the BOINC software infrastructure and have made it amenable for integration with the supercomputing and cloud computing environments. We have named the extension of the BOINC software infrastructure as BOINC@TACC [2], and are using it to route *qualified* HTC jobs from the supercomputers at the Texas Advanced Computing Center (TACC) to not only the typically volunteered devices but also to the cloud computing resources such as Jetstream [3] and Chameleon [4]. *We have developed a decision-support system for helping users determine whether or not their jobs are qualified for running through BOINC@TACC.* Depending upon the hardware requirements of the BOINC jobs, the routing scripts also determine if these jobs should be run in the cloud or on other volunteered resources.

A high-level overview of BOINC@TACC software infrastructure is shown in Fig. 1. As can be noticed from this Figure, running jobs through the BOINC@TACC software infrastructure involves Docker [5], which is a commonly used tool for the containerization of applications. Both community code and users' home-grown applications can be containerized and made portable across different hardware resources and environments by using Docker. As a new functionality, *we have developed a framework for automatically creating Docker images of user's home-grown code*, thereby, freeing them from the burden of climbing the learning curve for Docker and creating the Docker images of their applications. A complete overview of this system is available in Fig. 2 below.

Additionally, we have developed the software components for running BOINC jobs on the VMs in the cloud. These component can also be useful for cloud bursting [6] and routing not just the HTC jobs but also the High Performance Computing (HPC) jobs from the oversubscribed resources to the relatively underutilized systems at the supercomputing centers. In order *to support the cloud bursting mechanism, we have developed a new client software component for interacting with the BOINC server, and also a protocol for routing jobs and information between the new client and the BOINC server.*

The *BOINC@TACC software infrastructure has been made General Data Protection Regulation (GDPR)* [7] *compliant.* To ensure data privacy and security, our instance of the BOINC server is run on a private cloud computing infrastructure. For enabling TACC users in accessing BOINC@TACC through the project website, *we have also integrated the TACC user database with the BOINC@TACC software infrastructure.*

We are iteratively refining the BOINC@TACC infrastructure on the basis of the feedback from the researchers, volunteers, and the developers in the community. In the rest of this paper, we describe the details of the BOINC@TACC infrastructure. We also describe the process of submitting jobs to the BOINC server through the convenience of the web-browser or through the command-line interface. We include a description of the evaluation metrics, and future work. The BOINC@TACC infrastructure can be adapted by different supercomputing centers in their pursuit of multi-petascale (or even exascale computing).

2   Software and Implementation

The key software components in the BOINC@TACC infrastructure are its frontend (command-line and web-based), BOINC client-server, special client for supporting cloud bursting, framework for automatically creating Docker images of users' custom-code, Docker images of the popular community applications, scripts, APIs, databases, job taxonomy, accounting system, and email notification system. The majority of the implementation work required for this project was done using PHP/Javascript/HTML/CSS, Python, Bash scripts, Redis and MySQL database management systems.

We describe each of the aforementioned components in this section and provide an overview of the key software components/extensions that we have developed for integrating VC with supercomputing.

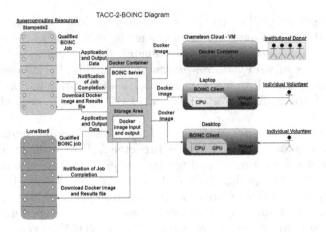

Fig. 1. BOINC@TACC project overview

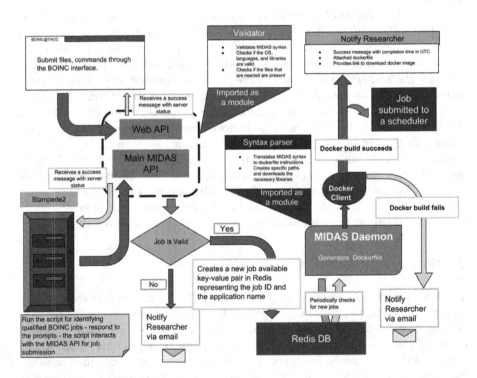

Fig. 2. MIDAS: Automatic dockerization via image, the system can be accessed both through the Stampede2 scripts or the web interface.

1. Front-End: The BOINC@TACC software infrastructure can be used for submitting jobs via two interfaces that were developed in the project: command-line and web-based. The command-line interface can be used on TACC supercomputers, and is basically a decision-support system that helps the users in determining whether their jobs are qualified for running through the BOINC@TACC infrastructure or not. If, as a part of the decision-making, it is determined that a job is not suitable for being routed to the BOINC server (perhaps because it is data-intensive or memory-intensive), then it is run directly on the TACC supercomputers. However, if a job is qualified for being routed to the BOINC server, there is further automatic decision-making involved to determine the type of resource on which the job should be scheduled, such as, a cloud computing resource or another volunteered resource that may be a laptop, desktop, or a tablet. Supporting cloud computing resources is especially important to meet the diverse hardware needs of the current TACC user-community. There is a high-demand for GPUs and some demand for FPGAs. The cloud computing resources can help in elastically supplementing the volunteered resources and provide new capabilities.
The web interface supports job submissions through the convenience of the web-browser, and mimics the functionality of the command-line interface. However, before a researcher can use the web interface, they are required to run a registration script from a TACC supercomputer (viz., Stampede2 or Lonestar5) and get validated. The registration scripts are organization specific and can only be run from TACC systems. The web interface can also be used to track the status of a submitted job or to access any other feature provided by BOINC.

2. Databases: There are two types of database management systems used in the BOINC@TACC software implementation: MySQL and Redis. BOINC provides a MySQL database by default. This database stores the information related to the volunteers' account, in addition to the job statistics, data related to the messageboards, volunteered devices, and the status of the jobs. We have made several changes to the default MySQL database to anonymize user information while maintaining the compatibility of the data with the existing software implementation. All usernames have been anonymized in compliance with GDPR and are stored as such in the database. No one other than the user and the administrator has access to the information related to user accounts. The users can choose to delete all the data, and we can guarantee its complete erasure from our systems.
Redis is an in-memory, key-value based database. It is used for data-caching and saving basic job information, such as job IDs and the image tags, while the complete information is stored in the MySQL database. Redis is also used for automatic Dockerfile construction, setting triggers that alert the internal daemon to begin the Docker build, and select the files to use. Redis is also used to store job classification tags for each job run.

3. BOINC client-server: The entire BOINC server architecture is composed of an Apache server, a MySQL database, and back-end programs/tools, and all of these components run as separate Docker containers [8] but are made to

start/stop together using Docker compose [9]. The project's state is made to persist using shared Docker volumes [10]. All the default features of BOINC (such as messageboards, job scheduler, and job statistics) have been maintained in the BOINC@TACC project. The default BOINC client, when installed on a volunteered device, automatically polls the server to check for available jobs, and runs them if the volunteered device is underutilized. The BOINC client also automatically returns the job results to the BOINC server. The client notifies the BOINC server if there are any errors while processing a job. Any job that fails to run due to the error on the volunteered hardware or software is considered as incomplete and is resubmitted.

One of the default requirements for running the Docker-based BOINC applications is the availability of VirtualBox on the volunteered resources. When the Docker containers are run inside the VirtualBox installed on the VMs in the cloud, they are unable to access the GPUs due to the hypervisor settings. While a Peripheral Component Interconnect (PCI) passthrough can be used to overcome this limitation, it is still in experimental stage, is difficult to set-up, and has strict hardware requirements that would make it difficult to uniformly use it on different volunteered resources. Moreover, on the Linux based resources/VMs, Docker containers can be run directly without requiring VirtualBox as long as Docker is installed. Therefore, in order to support Dockerized BOINC applications that need to access the GPUs, and to circumvent the requirement of installing VirtualBox on Linux-based resources (especially in the cloud), *we have developed the Automatic Docker Task Distribution Protocol (ADTD-P).*

ADTD-P relies on the availability of Docker on the VMs for running CPU jobs, and requires Nvidia Docker 2 package [11] for running GPU jobs that are submitted through the BOINC server. Using ADTD-P does not require any modification to the applications themselves. The functionality of ADTD-P is further described as follows:

1. On the server side, ADTD-P saves Docker images of the applications to be run as a BOINC job in a *tar.gz file. It then creates a JSON file with the information about the job, such as, whether or not it requires GPU support. The Docker image and the JSON file are compressed and saved together as a packet to be shipped as a BOINC job.

2. It should also be noted that ADTD-P is not exclusive for BOINC usage and can be used for submitting other types of volunteer jobs as long as they are packaged using docker images. Clients can also be made to avoid GPU jobs if the Nvidia Docker 2 package is not installed or CUDA jobs are not desired. We provide an automatic installer for ubuntu/debian systems.

3. When a job has completed - successfully or with a failure - the client will return a *tar.gz file containing the job information logs in a JSON format and the output files to the server. Both these files are then forwarded to the users. In case a job fails due to the issues not related to BOINC, the error logs are also sent to the users. The Docker container and the image used are then deleted from the client.

4. ADTD-P clients also maintain a database to locally track the jobs that they process. This information is stored in the Redis database connected to the ADTD-P server and contains processing times, commands run, job status, and job IDs. The job statistics can be directly retrieved from Redis, but ADTD-P also provides a command-line interface [12].

5. Docker images: We maintain Docker images of multiple community applications such as, Autodock-vina, GROMACS, and OpenSees in Docker Hub. Users can either choose to run these applications that are maintained by us, or provide Docker images created by them or someone else. We have also developed a framework for supporting automatic creation of Docker images from source code and this framework is known as MIDAS (the Multiple Input Docker Automation System). Users can use MIDAS either in the command-line mode or through the web interface to generate Docker images from their source code and specifications. The user may select the OS to be utilized and can also provide configuration options as they deem fit. Users are provided root access to the Docker image. If the image is built successfully, the researchers are notified via email and sent a copy of both the Dockerfile used to build the Docker image of their code, and a hyperlink to download the image. However, if the build fails, the researchers are notified and their job is not processed. To enable running the Docker images on volunteered resources, we use the boinc2docker tool [13]. This tool helps in transforming Docker images and their respective commands into a Virtual-Box application. A complete diagram of MIDAS functioning can be seen in Fig. 3 below.

6. Routing jobs from the BOINC server to the BOINC clients or directly to the VMs in the cloud: Jobs that the server processes using the boinc2docker tool are distributed to the volunteer devices using BOINC's default scheduler, which will select an appropriate volunteer host based on the job requirements (e.g., memory needs and the computation time required). Jobs submitted through the ADTD-P protocol, however, are processed on the First Come First Served (FCFS) basis, and are processed by the first ADTD-P client requesting a job. However, ADTD-P clients can have their own requirements, such as restricting GPU jobs.

7. Scripts for gathering results from the volunteered resources: BOINC jobs processed through BOINC's standard scheduler return the results using BOINC's default APIs through the BOINC client. These results are then added to a directory on the BOINC server. ADTD-P clients also return the results and a complete log of all executed commands to this directory.

8. Email notifications, job-tracking, and job statistics: We also support a job history page through which the researchers can track the status of the jobs submitted through the web interface. BOINC@TACC is also integrated with an email server for notifying the researchers about their jobs, results, and account information.

9. Job Classifier (Tagging): All jobs run using BOINC@TACC can be tagged - classified with none, one, or multiple science fields and subfields. Information about these tags is stored in a Redis database.

10. Accounting System: This system can be used by the organizations to check and limit the allocation of compute time and storage space for the researchers using volunteered resources. When a user signs up, allocation gets automatically assigned according to the parameters set by the organization. More than one organization can be served by a BOINC server instance and each one may provide different storage requirements and permissions to its users. In order for an individual to use the BOINC@TACC functionality, they must belong to an allowed organization which is TACC.

11. Information and System Security: Only researchers with both valid TACC credentials and an active TACC allocation are allowed to submit jobs through BOINC@TACC. Once a user has registered for BOINC@TACC project by running a script (provided by us), the system will automatically generate a token for him/her. This token is used to internally map the users and the jobs submitted by them.

The BOINC@TACC project is GDPR compliant. To comply with GDPR, as a default setting, it was important to anonymize the volunteers' data presented on the leaderboard accessible through the web interface. If users wish to, and give their explicit consent, we can easily display their chosen screennames instead of the anonymized names. GDPR also mandates presenting the terms and conditions for joining the project in the simplest possible manner. The project team keeps track of all the places where the volunteers' data is kept so that in the event the volunteers need to delete their accounts, all their information can be deleted with certainty. This feature however may need to be rethought/reworked once the project is integrated with the Science United web application [14] in the future.

The default BOINC APIs sanitize all files submitted to ensure that there are no hidden commands within the file-names. The BOINC@TACC server is deployed on a private VMWare cloud computing system instead of Jetstream for reliability, security, and to ensure access to TACC's internal LDAP server. By default, the usage of bots to automatically run BOINC jobs is permitted and encouraged for users who have large computing systems and wish to do so. All users wishing to become volunteers and allow BOINC to compute on their devices will be required to pass a CAPTCHA test when signing up for the very first time.

3   Job Submission Workflow

Any researcher or scholar wishing to submit jobs using the BOINC@TACC framework must possess TACC credentials and a valid allocation. All prospective users are required to execute the registration script through either Lonestar5 or Stampede2 before being able to use the web interface. Researcher login is integrated with TACC's LDAP server in order to ensure appropriate access to computer resources.

We maintain a set of Docker images of popular community code (e.g., Autodock-Vina, GROMACS, NAMD, and OpenSees). A researcher/scholar can choose to run any of these with their input files/commands on volunteered resources while interacting with the BOINC@TACC infrastructure through the command-line interface or through the web interface. A screen-shot of the web interface is shown in Fig. 3, and the scripts for using BOINC@TACC from the command-line interface have been made available through a Github repository [15].

Job Submission

Location of docker image *	◉ List of docker images maintained by BOINC@TACC ○ Docker hub ○ Automated docker build

List of docker images maintained by BOINC@TACC ▾

List of commands *

e.g., gcc -o hello.exe hello.c (hit enter at each of the end the command line including the last command line)

Input files *   ◉ Tar Upload   ○ Zip Upload   ○ No Input Files

Browse   No file chosen

Submit the job

(*) required

Fig. 3. Web interface for BOINC job submission.

Additionally, instead of choosing to run the applications whose Docker images are maintained by us, researchers/scholars can provide any public Docker Hub image along with the input files/commands to run.

BOINC@TACC also provides an automated process of creating custom Docker images from the source code for users who do not have existing Docker images of their custom-written/home-grown code. This process involves using the MIDAS software component. We support building Docker images of applications written in C, C++, Fortran, Python, R, and bash. These new images can contain any number of data files as well. The jobs submitted through the command-line interface on Stampede2/Lonestar5, but not qualified to run on volunteered resources, are automatically submitted to the SLURM scheduler on Stampede2/Lonestar5.

4   Backend Workflow

After job submission, the job information (user information, image used, commands, and input files) is relayed to the BOINC server where any required pre-processing is done (such as downloading data from a third-party server or converting the source-code to a Docker image).

The server automatically accesses the images supported by us without requiring any detailed user input. If a user selects to run a third-party image from Docker Hub, the BOINC@TACC system will prompt the user to specify appropriate tags for their jobs. MIDAS jobs - or those jobs for which the user needs help in generating Docker images - must be specified using a particular syntax. To the best of our knowledge, no other BOINC project supports the feature of automatically creating Docker images from source-code and user-specifications.

Most BOINC@TACC jobs are processed using the boinc2docker tool and are made available to the BOINC scheduler directly. The BOINC scheduler selects an available volunteered device based on the job characteristics, such as the memory and I/O requirements. The devices running BOINC clients are expected to have VirtualBox installed. The Docker image runs inside the Docker container, which in turn runs in the VirtualBox connected via BOINC client.

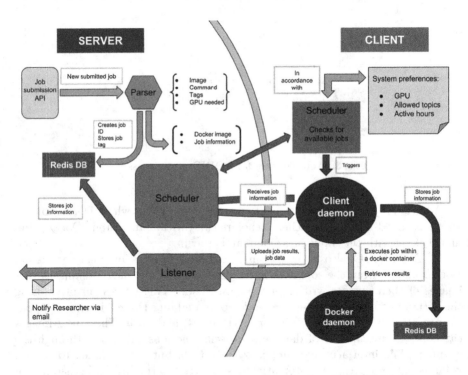

Fig. 4. MIDAS: ADTD-P system as implemented in BOINC@TACC.

BOINC@TACC is also integrated with a secondary job submission framework: the Automated Docker Task Distribution Protocol (ADTD-P). ADTD-P does not require VirtualBox and is only dependant on Docker for CPU-only jobs. It requires CUDA drivers and the Nvidia Docker 2 package for CUDA GPU jobs. When an ADTD-P job is available, a client running on Jetstream or Chameleon downloads the Docker image, loads it, and executes the commands inside a Docker container. If the job is successful, it collects the results and uploads them to the BOINC server. It also logs all the job processing details. A pictorial overview of the ADTD-P framework is shown in Fig. 4.

When a job is completed, the BOINC client notifies the BOINC server, which then sends an email message to the researcher/scholar along with the link to download the package containing the output files. The researchers/scholars can also monitor the status of their job through the BOINC@TACC project website: http://boinc.tacc.utexas.edu/ (login as a researcher is required). All jobs submitted through BOINC@TACC are tagged, and the data related to the tags will be used in future to integrate the project with the Science United project so that the volunteers can choose the projects that they wish to support more easily.

5 Scalability

The BOINC@TACC system can elastically scale-up to support HTC jobs by harnessing the VMs running in the cloud. In comparison to a regular server or container clusters, the number of jobs run through BOINC@TACC can become virtually infinite as long as volunteers provide devices to execute the computation.

All user data and results are stored on a Docker volume mounted on the host for data persistence. This container can also be run on a different server in order to reduce the disk space requirements of the main server. Information credentials for passing information between the BOINC server and the storage server (named as Reef) are not shared directly with the users for security purposes. Furthermore, all communication and files passed to storage must go through the BOINC server.

6 Challenges and Lessons Learnt

- Data anonymization: For GDPR Compliance, we initially added a new column to the MySQL database for storing the anonymized volunteer names. This created issues related to inconsistent display of volunteer information across the project website. BOINC recognizes only the default structure of the MySQL database, which does not contain anonymized names. To fix this issue, we created a new table that only stores the anonymized user name for each user's screen name.
- Emails: Users are sent results attached to an email and a link for future downloads is provided. Gmail was used in the early stages but it was discontinued in favor of GNU Mailman because Gmail has storage limits and Google can shut-down Gmail accounts that send automated mails to discourage any spam-related activity.
- VirtualBox installation: It was not possible to use VirtualBox on the VMs available to us due to a communication issue between the BOINC client and VirtualBox for running GPU jobs. ADTD-P was created to run BOINC jobs directly in the VMs without using VirtualBox.

- Nvidia GPU access through Docker: Regular Docker containers do not have access to an Nvidia GPU even when the necessary drivers and CUDA services have been installed. As a result, ADTD-P clients were built using the Nvidia Docker 2 package. This allows containers to run CUDA jobs without any extra setup, while retaining the same functionality and syntax of a regular Docker job.

7 Limitations

One of the main limitations of VC is the volatility in the availability of the volunteered resources, and their performance. While the users are guaranteed a certain level of performance when running applications on supercomputers, they may experience unpredictable performance when running on volunteered resources. A lot of the supercomputer users run memory-intensive and IO-intensive applications which are not a good-fit for the VC environment. A lot of the jobs run at the supercomputing centers are based on distributed-memory paradigm, and such jobs are also not a right fit for the VC model.

8 Evaluation

We are in the process of evaluating the BOINC@TACC project in terms of the job turnaround time, the number of jobs submitted, the number of jobs that run successfully, and the number of volunteers and researchers that are interested in using the project.

As the project is in its early stages of community building, currently, we have only about 65 volunteers and researchers who are being serviced through the BOINC@TACC project, and this number will likely increase with future community building efforts. We have not opened the system to unknown researchers.

We selected popular community code for our testing and evaluation: AutoDock Vina [16] from the computational biology domain, Opensees [17] from the earthquake simulation engineering domain, and three applications from the molecular dynamics domain - NAMD [18], LAMMPS [19], GROMACS [20]. These applications were submitted through the BOINC@TACC command-line interface available on the Stampede2 supercomputer. We also ran these applications directly on the Skylake nodes on the Stampede2 supercomputer at TACC. The Skylake nodes are high-end as compared to the processors on the volunteered resources, and as can be noticed from the data in Table 2, the performance of the applications on Stampede2 was better than their performance on the volunteered resources. As we did not experience any queue wait time at the time of running these test jobs, the job turn-around time on the volunteered resources is longer than the time on Stampede2 (please see Table 1). However, the queue wait time on Stampede2 is a highly unpredictable characteristic that depends upon the other users who are simultaneously using the system. When Stampede2 is down for maintenance or has a large back-log of pending jobs, the turn-around time from the volunteered resources could be shorter than that of Stampede2.

Table 1. Comparing job turn-around time (email sending time not included)

Application name	Image size	Stampede2 Skylake node -4 cores requested	BOINC@TACC	
			Boinc2docker (VirtualBox in 4-core volunteer)	ADTD-P (Jestream cloud server, 6 cores, 4 used)
Autodock-Vina	697 MB	30 s	6 min 32 s	8 min 30 s
OpenSees	1.331 GB	5 s	3 min 19 s	10 min 18 s
NAMD	288 MB	5 s	15 min 47 s	3 min 22 s
LAMMPS	1.47 GB	3 s	3 h 14 min 19 s	12 min 13 s
GROMACS	1.27 GB	8 s	3 h 8 min 34 s	11 min 58 s

Table 2. Comparing the computation time spent

Application name	Image size	Stampede2 Skylake node -4 cores requested	BOINC@TACC	
			Boinc2docker (VirtualBox in 4-core volunteer)	ADTD-P (Jestream cloud server, 6 cores, 4 used)
Autodock-Vina	697 MB	28 s	5 min 21 s	1 min 9 s
OpenSees	1.331 GB	3 s	2 min 44 s	<1 s
NAMD	288 MB	<1 s	23 s	2 s
LAMMPS	1.47 GB	3 s	1 min 45 s	<1 s
GROMACS	1.27 GB	<1 s	1 min 38 s	<1 s

9 Related Work

There are multiple VC projects in the community that are using BOINC for harnessing the power of the donated compute-cycles. These projects are typically deployed by the research groups for running specific applications to solve very specific research problems that are related to their interest. Contrary to the objective of other VC projects in the community that run niche applications, the BOINC@TACC project is designed to cater to the computing needs of a wide range of TACC users from different research domains, and hence, supports running arbitrary applications in Docker containers.

10 Future Work

All current BOINC logs about submitted jobs are stored in MySQL by the scheduler, and in an additional Redis database for internal server mapping. However, as mentioned above, Redis is an in-memory database and is not designed for large job logs. Instead, InfluxDB is a better choice for handling large amounts of time-series data, and will be used in the next iteration of the BOINC@TACC software release. The Grafana interface [21] will also be added to facilitate administrative overview of job statistics. Currently, the main BOINC server automatically generates the Docker image using the MIDAS client locally. It also packages and archives all ADTD-P information locally. This could become a problem when an extremely large set of jobs is submitted, since it becomes a bottleneck to job processing. In the future software releases, we will improve the scalability of our software.

11   Conclusion

In the paper we presented an introduction to the BOINC@TACC project, and discussed the advantages of unifying supercomputing with volunteer computing and cloud computing. We explained that the BOINC@TACC project can potentially help users in supplementing their allocation of compute-time on the TACC supercomputers, especially because there are roughly 500,000 devices in the community that are already actively participating in the VC projects. Some of these devices are equipped with modern GPUs. More than 100 volunteers have already signed-up for the BOINC@TACC project.

We also discussed the need for harnessing the available computing power through the cloud computing systems hosted by TACC so that if there is a spike in the demand for the computing power, or need for special hardware that is not available on the other volunteered resources, we can still service the jobs submitted through BOINC@TACC with a reasonable guarantee for the quality of service. The software infrastructure for the BOINC@TACC project is being iteratively refined and released to the public. Other supercomputing and cloud computing service providers can conveniently adapt and adopt the BOINC@TACC software infrastructure for their environments.

Acknowledgement. The BOINC@TACC project is funded through National Science Foundation (NSF) award # 1664022. We are grateful to XSEDE, TACC, and the Science Gateway Community Institute for providing the resources required for implementing this project. We are grateful to David Anderson, Thomas Johnson, and Anubhaw Nand for contributing to the BOINC@TACC codebase and their contribution in preparing this paper. Figure 1 was prepared by Thomas Johnson. Several results presented in this paper were obtained using the Chameleon testbed supported by the NSF and we are grateful to NSF for the same.

References

1. Anderson, D.P.: BOINC: a system for public-resource computing and storage. In: Fifth IEEE/ACM International Workshop on Grid Computing (2004)
2. BOINC@TACC (2018). http://boinc.tacc.utexas.edu/. Accessed 26 Oct 2018
3. Jetstream (2018). https://use.jetstream-cloud.org/. Accessed 26 Oct 2018
4. Chameleon. https://www.chameleoncloud.org/. Accessed 26 Oct 2018
5. Docker. https://www.docker.com/. Accessed 26 Oct 2018

6. Cloud   Bursting.   https://azure.microsoft.com/en-us/overview/what-is-cloud-bursting/. Accessed 26 Oct 2018
7. GDPR   Compliance.   https://ec.europa.eu/info/law/law-topic/data-protection/reform/rules-business-and-organisations_en. Accessed 26 Oct 2018
8. Docker Containers. https://www.docker.com/resources/what-container. Accessed 26 Oct 2018
9. Docker Compose. https://docs.docker.com/compose/overview/. Accessed 26 Oct 2018
10. Docker Volumes. https://docs.docker.com/storage/volumes/. Accessed 26 Oct 2018
11. NVIDIA Docker Github Repo. https://github.com/NVIDIA/nvidia-docker. Accessed 26 Oct 2018
12. ADTD-P Protocol Github Repo. https://github.com/noderod/adtd-protocol/blob/master/history.py. Accessed 26 Oct 2018
13. BOINC2Docker Github Repo. https://github.com/marius311/boinc2docker. Accessed 26 Oct 2018
14. Science United. https://scienceunited.org/. Accessed 26 Oct 2018
15. BOINC@TACC Github Repo. https://github.com/ritua2/BOINCatTACC. Accessed 26 Oct 2018
16. Trott, O., Olson, A.J.: AutoDock Vina: improving the speed and accuracy of docking with a new scoring function, efficient optimization and multithreading. J. Comput. Chem. **31**(2), 455–461 (2010)
17. Opensees. http://opensees.berkeley.edu/. Accessed 26 Oct 2018
18. Phillips, J.C., et al.: Scalable molecular dynamics with NAMD. J. Comput. Chem. **26**, 1781–1802 (2005)
19. Plimpton, S.: Fast parallel algorithms for short-range molecular dynamics. J. Comput. Phys. **117**, 1–19 (1995)
20. Berendsen, H.J.C., Drunen, R.V., Spoel, D.V.D.: GROMACS: a message-passing parallel molecular dynamics implementation. Comput. Phys. Commun. **91**, 43–56 (1995)
21. Grafana. http://docs.grafana.org/features/datasources/influxdb/. Accessed 26 Oct 2018

High-Productivity Tools and Frameworks

High-Level Approaches for Leveraging Deep-Memory Hierarchies on Modern Supercomputers

Antonio Gómez-Iglesias[1][(✉)] and Ritu Arora[2]

[1] Intel Corporation, Hillsboro, USA
antoniogi@gmail.com
[2] Texas Advanced Computing Center, The University of Texas at Austin, Austin, USA
rauta@tacc.utexas.edu

Abstract. There is a growing demand for supercomputers that can support memory-intensive applications to solve large-scale problems from various domains. Novel supercomputers with fast and complex memory subsystems are being provisioned to meet this demand. While complex and deep-memory hierarchies offer increased memory-bandwidth they can also introduce additional latency. Optimizing the memory usage of the applications is required to improve performance. However, this can be an effort-intensive and a time-consuming activity if done entirely manually. Hence, high-level approaches for supporting the memory-management and memory-optimization on modern supercomputers are needed. Such scalable approaches can contribute towards supporting the users at the open-science data centers - mostly domain scientists and students - in their code modernization efforts. In this paper, we present a memory management and optimization workflow based on high-level tools. While the workflow can be generalized for supercomputers with different architectures, we demonstrate its usage on the Stampede2 system at the Texas Advanced Computing Center that contains both Intel Knights Landing and Intel Xeon processors, and each Knights Landing node offers both DDR4 and MCDRAM.

1 Introduction

Performance of the memory system/sub-system often does not match the computational capability of the latest processing elements that are available in modern supercomputers. Even though the single core performance does not continue to grow as it did in the previous decades, the number of cores per processor have gone up with a decrease in the clock frequency of those cores. This comes from the fact that dynamic power requirements for a transistor depends on the energy of a logic transition multiplied by the frequency of transitions [5].

The continuous growth in computing capabilities in existing and upcoming supercomputers has led to a memory bottleneck. Memory technologies (DDR to

© Springer Nature Singapore Pte Ltd. 2019
A. Majumdar and R. Arora (Eds.): SCEC 2018, CCIS 964, pp. 123–139, 2019.
https://doi.org/10.1007/978-981-13-7729-7_9

DDR4) have improved to offer more bandwidth. However, the growth rate for the memory has not been able to keep up with the growth in computing capabilities of the cores in the chip. This has meant that the memory bandwidth per core has decreased. While several High Performance Computing (HPC) applications benefit from the higher FLOPS that the modern compute nodes provide, there are several other memory-intensive applications (e.g., image processing applications [4] and Deep Neural Networks) that still suffer from the limited memory-bandwidth.

In order to address the memory-bandwidth issue, the manufactures are designing chips that have High Bandwidth Memory (HBM) [8] integrated "on package". The most recent self-bootable Intel Xeon Phi generation (Knights Landing - KNL) cards are packed with 16 GB of HBM that is named as MCDRAM (Multi-Channel DRAM - Intel's proprietary memory). The MCDRAM can be configured either as a third-level cache or as a NUMA (Non-Uniform Memory Access) node, and up to 384 GB of DDR4 memory. With the specification of HBM2 already defined, along with the fact that the HBM3 specifications ensuring higher memory-bandwidth than HBM2 have already been outlined by some manufacturers, it is clear that HBM/HBM2/HBM3 will continue to feature in the next generation supercomputers. In addition to HBM, some of the latest supercomputers also incorporate another level in the memory hierarchy in the form of Non-Volatile RAM (NVRAM). This further expands the possibilities of addressing the memory bandwidth needs of the users along with increasing the complexity of the system and, potentially making an application complex when trying to reach peak performance.

Based on the recent trends in large-scale HPC systems, and despite the fact that Intel has discontinued its KNL product-line, we consider that the KNL chip is a good representation of the complexity in the design of processors in current and future generation supercomputers. The KNL chip (or package) has: (1) many-core architecture where each core runs at a relatively low frequency and implements several simplifications over other Intel Xeon chips in order to meet power requirements [20]; (2) contained power consumption; and (3) different types of memories that satisfy different requirements (large capacity - low bandwidth; limited capacity - higher bandwidth). The inclusion of different types of addressable memory in a package increases its overall complexity and it is not a straightforward task to efficiently harness its capabilities. The memory-intensive applications running on such packages need to be adapted to achieve the best possible performance. Without these modifications, such applications will see an increased execution time and an overall reduction of the efficient utilization of the resources.

When running applications on systems with deep-memory hierarchies, it is important to analyze the memory usage characteristics of the applications, and determine the memory layers in which the applications' data structures should reside. This, however, can be a challenging task for many software developers. Moreover, different supercomputers target different communities: some systems are designed to meet the requirements of a handful of users and applications [3], while other machines are conceived with the aim of supporting large number of users, collaborations [15, 22] and applications. In the latter, users of these systems are often either domain experts or graduate students who are using such complex systems for the first time. Often times, these users do not have the skills or time to adapt their applications to take advantage of the latest features on the supercomputers. Therefore, high-level tools for memory-usage optimization on modern supercomputers are needed. Such tools can significantly reduce the amount of effort and time required for optimizing the applications. While these tools might not reach the performance that advanced and expert users would be able to attain, they should still be able to adapt the applications to obtain a significant percentage of the peak performance.

In this paper, we present a workflow based on high-levels tools for helping users in taking advantage of the deep-memory hierarchies without knowing the low-level microarchitectural details. The workflow is designed for usage on production-quality supercomputers and is already available on petascale systems used by thousands of users worldwide [21]. The tools can work in the user-space without the need of privileged access. This simplifies the implementation of the workflow on many production systems. The results presented in this paper demonstrate the value-addition done by our workflow during the process of memory-usage optimization. The rest of this paper is organized as follows: Sect. 2 introduces the related work; Sect. 3 details the overall workflow and the tools involved in its implementation. Section 4 introduces a set of benchmarks and real applications that were used for getting the results presented in this same section. Finally, Sect. 5 summarizes the main findings of the paper and introduces our future work.

2   Related Work

RTHMS [13] is a tool that analyzes parallel applications and provides a set of recommendations regarding data placement on systems with different types of memory. This work is similar to the work done by [11] in the sense that both define a metric for placing data structures on the HBM (MCDRAM). They both analyze whether a data structure fits in the available memory so that it can be fully allocated in it. RTHMS also considers some memory access patterns, which makes it a more advanced option. Such tools optimize the applications at compile time, and while they are useful, they can potentially mispredict the data structures that should be placed on the HBM since they lack critical information that only exists at run-time, like size of the dynamically allocated data structures.

Authors in [2] propose a runtime system that automatically moves data to and from MCDRAM on KNL when needed using the Charm++ runtime system. It, however, needs the users and programmers to annotate the code to describe which data structures might be bandwidth-sensitive. This is an effort that many users are either not willing to undertake or they cannot afford.

Both the aforementioned efforts focus on a particular part of the problem that we have described in Sect. 1 of the paper. Advanced users can use these approaches or they can use any of the available profilers to extract the information required for identifying the data structures that should be allocated on the HBM. Based on our experience, it can be stated that such advanced users rarely rely on new tools that simply act as an additional layer on top of the tools that they can already use. However, for not so advanced users, these tools still do not hide enough hardware complexity to make them useful.

Arora et al. developed a tool [1] to guide the users in compiling and running their applications efficiently on KNL nodes. The tool can also be used to interactively adapt codes developed in C/C++/Fortran to selectively allocate certain data structures used in the application on the MCDRAM. The authors mention extending the tool to support advance vectorization and provide advanced options for memory-usage optimization as part of their future work.

Rosales et al. [18] presented a tool that monitors the utilization of hardware resources on supercomputers by a given application with a very low overhead. This tool is in production on a number of supercomputers with thousands of users having access to it. It allows users to gather information about a vast number of resources available on a compute node. It also offers a summarized and a simple overview of the main issues that an application can be suffering from while running on a supercomputer.

3   Memory Management and Optimization Workflow

We present a user-friendly memory management and optimization workflow for applications running on modern supercomputers. The workflow can be adapted and adopted for future exascale systems as well. It consists of a set of tools for analyzing the application characteristics, especially those related to memory utilization. Users are not required to perform any manual re-engineering of their applications.

Our recommended workflow is diagrammatically shown in Fig. 1 and the steps labelled in this Figure are explained in the following subsections. For simplicity and reproducibility, we are going to describe the implementation of the workflow on a supercomputer consisting of KNL nodes. We use a collection of external tools, libraries, hardware/performance counters, and the data in `sysfs`. All the steps in our workflow run in user-space, without the need for privileged permissions, to ensure portability and to simplify adoption. We expect that this workflow can be adapted for other chips with deep-memory hierarchies since those chips are very likely to have similar libraries and tools too.

3.1   Identify Memory Requirements

As shown in Fig. 1, the first step of our workflow consists of identifying the memory requirements of the target application. This step applies to all the compute nodes used during run-time. The information that we collect per node includes:

- Memory used by the application: if the application consists of several other applications running on the same node, which is a typical case for many

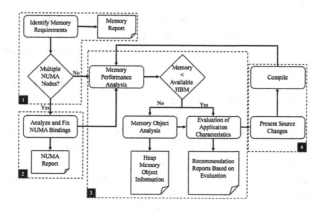

Fig. 1. Overall workflow. It consists of four different stages with reports after each step to ensure that users can make informed decisions regarding memory management and optimization.

workflows or in Multiple Instruction, Multiple Data (MIMD) scenarios, we collect the overall memory footprint. We also consider that the actual memory used by an application includes both virtual memory and the ramdisk in /dev/shm since that also counts towards the main memory utilization.

- Free memory: capturing the memory used by an application can be difficult or the data might not be completely accurate under some scenarios. As a result, we also collect the information on the amount of memory available at all times during the application run-time. This value can provide a better insight in cases where the out-of-memory killer terminates the execution of the target application.
- NUMA utilization: similar to tracking main memory utilization, when NUMA is present, the utilization of each NUMA node is captured. This can be used to quickly detect NUMA affinity problems in NUMA-aware applications or NUMA problems in unoptimized applications.
- NUMA statistics: we collect the number of NUMA hits and misses and whether the hits or misses are local or remote. This information is important to later on analyze how NUMA-aware the code is and to decide if the code can be modified to improve the performance.

At this step of the workflow, if there is only one NUMA domain, step 2 is skipped since that stage of the workflow focuses on fixing the NUMA bindings.

3.2   Analyze NUMA Utilization and Fix NUMA Bindings

In the previous step, we collected information about NUMA utilization as well as a set of NUMA counters. This information is analyzed and presented to the users so that they decide whether to continue with the workflow or to stop. This step of the workflow does not introduce code modifications, but rather helps users with an easy approach to improve the NUMA bindings of their applications.

As previously stated, we are using the Intel KNL processor to demonstrate our recommended workflow. This processor supports different *cluster modes* [20], that are basically boot-time configurations, to expose the available MCDRAM as different NUMA nodes. In some of the cluster modes (all-to-all, hemisphere and quadrant), the MCDRAM is configured as a single NUMA node. However, there are other modes (sub-NUMA, or SNC 2 or 4) where the MCDRAM is configured as 2 or 4 different NUMA nodes.

If the MCDRAM is configured in sub-NUMA 2 or 4 mode, the operating system will see the available MCDRAM as 2 or 4 NUMA nodes (and also, it will see 2 or 4 NUMA nodes for the DDR4 memory, resulting in 4 or 8 total NUMA nodes). Even though there is no physical distinction between the hardware based on how it is configured in software, as it is still the same chip, the mechanism for data access changes. Accessing data that is not located on the memory controller of the local NUMA domain [20] imposes a latency penalty in the same way as accessing remote memory on a multi-socket system.

The workflow generates a set of plots that represent the NUMA utilization during the execution of the target application. The information on NUMA utilization is collected using the numastat tool. These plots include the memory available and used on each NUMA node (which considers all NUMA nodes independent of their level in the hierarchy), the local NUMA hits and misses, as well as the remote hits and misses. The visualization of the results gives a very quick idea of where problems reside at run-time.

This step of the workflow is required for those applications whose memory footprint makes them suitable for running entirely within a subset of the NUMA nodes. In systems with deep-memory hierarchies, different NUMA nodes will present different characteristics (i.e., some nodes will have HBM). There are different options for using the different levels in the hierarchy. If the memory requirements of an application can be met by the HBM, then all the data structures needed by the application can be created there. Typically, numactl is used to achieve this.

In cases where there is a single NUMA node for each type of memory in the hierarchy, using the numactl tool with the appropriate flags is sufficient to specify which NUMA node must be used first. The problem arises when there are multiple NUMA nodes for each type of memory in the hierarchy. In this case, setting the correct policy with numactl is more complicated if the target application has been parallelized with MPI. Consider the scenario where, in one node, the application is executed as mpirun ./target_app and the memory hierarchy of the node consists of DDR4 and HBM. There are two sockets in the node, and each socket has its own local DDR4 and HBM memory. In this case, there are two NUMA nodes for DDR4 and another two for the HBM. Also in this case, suppose that the two DDR4 NUMA nodes are nodes 0 and 1, while the HBM nodes are 2 and 3. By default, the application would run out of DDR4. However, if the user introduces numactl to set the memory bindings to use HBM, the application will use one of the two HBM nodes until full and then use the other HBM node. This can happen by using the following command: mpirun numactl --membind=2,3

./target_app. However, there will still be NUMA misses. We introduce a tool that detects and fixes the CPU affinity of each individual MPI task at runtime. Based on that CPU affinity, it instructs numactl to set the memory policy to use the local NUMA nodes by default. Also, we use the preferred option for numactl, so that the application would use first the *local* HBM NUMA node and then, when all the HBM is completely used, it would allocate memory on the local DDR4 node. This tool can be configured to select which one of the local nodes to use. Our approach is independent of the MPI library used to compile/run the application and does not need any additional configurations. Thus, the command looks like mpirun fix_affinity ./target_app.

At this point, if the memory footprint of a given application is smaller than the available HBM, the workflow ends. However, if the memory access pattern of the given application is latency-sensitive instead of bandwidth-sensitive or the memory footprint is larger than the capacity provided by the HBM, there are additional steps in the workflow.

3.3   Identify Bandwidth-Critical Data Structures

As shown in Fig. 1, the third step while analyzing applications for improving performance is to identify the bandwidth-critical data that can reside on the HBM (or MCDRAM) instead of the DDR4. One of the tools in our workflow, named **ICAT** [1], can be used to analyze the application characteristics for identifying this data. ICAT runs the target application and gathers the information on microarchitectural events - such as instructions per cycle, L1 cache loads, L1 cache stores, L1 cache load misses, L1 cache store misses, Last Level Cache (LLC) loads, LLC cache stores, LLC cache load misses, and LLC cache store misses. It also collects the information on the fraction of cycles for which the processor was stalled on the different levels of cache and the DRAM. If needed, the tool computes the total sizes of the memory objects in an application, and the memory access patterns (such as strided access) by internally using hardware performance counters, software profiles, and built-in heuristics. These heuristics are related to: (1) size of the data structures, (2) the number of accesses, (3) whether or not the data structures are memory bound, (4) whether or not the data structures are DRAM bound, and (5) the amount of memory needed by the entire application. If the application fits into L2 cache then flat-mode with default settings is recommended and the memory allocation is done on DDR4. Otherwise, ICAT checks if the application fits in MCDRAM and numactl is available - if numactl is available, then flat-mode with all allocation to MCDRAM is recommended but if numactl is not available, then cache-mode is recommended with a warning of performance-penalty. Using the aforementioned information and metrics, ICAT does the analysis for decision-making purposes. On the basis of its analysis, it guides the users in prioritizing the allocation of memory objects on the HBM[1].

---

[1] https://colfaxresearch.com/knl-mcdram/.

As mentioned in Sect. 3.2, the KNL nodes can be configured in different *memory* and *cluster* modes, and the performance of an application can be impacted by the choice of these modes [17]. While there are some default configurations of these modes recommended by Intel, one would need to understand the memory usage characteristics of a given application to determine the most suitable modes to use for running it. There can be some trial-and-error involved in this process, and tools like Vtune [16] could be required to understand the memory usage pattern of a given application. Understanding the output of Vtune and making the decision on the appropriate modes to use can be difficult for many supercomputer users. Such users can take advantage of the decision-support tool that is incorporated in our workflow. Our tool already analyzes the aforementioned microarchitectural characteristics of a given serial or parallel application to advise on bandwidth-critical data structures and it can also recommend the best KNL configuration modes for running a given application. It prepares the recommendation reports for the user and also advises on the appropriate usage of the numactl options.

3.4   Iterative Code Adaptation for Optimizing Memory Use

The applications running on KNL processors that have the MCDRAM configured as an L3 cache are not required to undergo any change. However, if the MCDRAM is configured in flat-mode, as an extension of the DDR4 memory address space, the users can choose to allocate memory for specific bandwidth-critical data structures on the MCDRAM using the hbwmalloc interface, and thereby, gain some performance [7]. ICAT can determine if there are bandwidth-critical data structures that should be allocated to the MCDRAM. It can not only inform the user but can also re-engineer the code to use the hbwmalloc interface [7] for dynamic memory allocation in C, C++, and Fortran applications. The main changes required for updating an application to use the hbwmalloc interface include: (1) adding an include statement for a header file; (2) allocating memory dynamically for the bandwidth-critical data structures by using the hbw_malloc call that is available through the hbwmalloc interface instead of calling the malloc function; and (3) updating calls to the function free with the calls to the hbw_free function. However, additional lines of code are required if it is desired to make the application portable across systems that do not contain MCDRAM. ICAT can re-engineer a given application for optimally using the MCDRAM and adds the necessary checks in the code so that the application does not fail when it is run on systems that do not contain MCDRAM or do not have the memkind library [7].

ICAT has a very light-weight parser, code analyzer, and code translator written in C++ and bash for identifying certain grammar rules and patterns in the applications written using the following base languages: C, C++, and Fortran. ICAT can handle ambiguities in the C++ language on the basis of the context. ICAT works with 100% accuracy for code adaptation. Code modification at few places may not be hard to do manually. However, manually (1) writing portable code that is easy to maintain and run on systems that may or may not have MCDRAM, and (2) identifying potential candidates for allocation on MCDRAM can be difficult for several domain scientists and students - the target audience of our tools and workflow. These are the situations in which ICAT is the most valuable.

It should be noted that ICAT is not fully automatic. While it is capable of (1) identifying the data structures that are appropriate candidates for allocation on MCDRAM, and (2) making appropriate code changes for allocating those data structures on the MCDRAM, it relies on user-guidance to shortlist the data structures that should be allocated on MCDRAM. It produces a report on all the data structures that are good candidates for allocation on MCDRAM. It then iteratively prompts the user to agree or disagree to allocate those data structures on MCDRAM. Only when the user agrees to the suggestions made by the tool, the tool makes the changes to the code.

4 Experimental Set up and Results

We implemented and tested our workflow on the KNL nodes in the Stampede2 supercomputer [21]. The KNL nodes offer a memory-bandwidth of up to 479 GB/s when using MCDRAM directly, while this value decreases to 85 GB/s in the case of DDR4 [19]. We measured the run-time of our benchmarks using different configuration modes of the KNL nodes, and present an analysis of the results. While hard to quantify, we also demonstrate that our workflow raises the level of abstraction of using systems with deep-memory hierarchies.

4.1 Selected Benchmarks

We have selected a set of benchmarks that are representative of common workloads on supercomputers at several open-science data centers. We have focused on applications that are easily available and that also allow replication of our experiments with the arguments and configurations that we detail in this section. All codes were compiled with the -O3 and -xMIC-AVX512 flags:

1. MiniMD [6] is a parallel molecular dynamics simulation code and is part of the Mantevo project [12]. It computes physical properties like energy and pressure for a simulated space containing atoms. We focus on the MPI+OpenMP version of the code. We used Intel MPI 17.0.3 and Intel Compiler 17.0.4. We chose a problem size of 64^3, atomic density of 0.8442, 200 timesteps and performed reneighboring after every 10 steps. The experiments were carried out on a single Intel KNL node, with 8 MPI processes and 8 threads per process. The OpenMP affinity was set to spread. Finally, we set OMP_PLACES to threads, so that each OpenMP thread can be assigned to individual hardware threads on the target machine.

2. MiniFE [6] is another mini application that is also part of the Mantevo benchmark suite. It mimics the implementation of finite element generation, assembly, and solution for unstructured grid problems. It works over a 3-D box,

with the dimensions of the box being passed as arguments. The implementation supports both MPI and OpenMP. We selected the optimized hybrid version for KNL, both with and without `memkind` support [7]. For our runs, we used a 3-D box of size 256^3. The code was executed using 16 MPI tasks and 4 OpenMP threads on a KNL node. Similar to MiniMD, we set `OMP_PLACES` to `threads` and used a `spread` affinity for the threads.

3. SPPARKS [14] is a Monte Carlo application that can be run using any of the following algorithms: Kinetic Monte Carlo (KMC), rejection KMC (rKMC), and Metropolis Monte Carlo (MMC). There are multiple subcategories of SPPARKS applications and the supported computational models. For our experiments, we chose to run an Ising model. The region for the problem is a block of sizes [0,500] and [0,500]. We simulated the problem for 100 s, setting a random sweep. Since the code is a pure MPI code, we ran it with 1 MPI task per physical core of the KNL node (total of 68 tasks).

4. LULESH (Livermore Unstructured Lagrange Explicit Shock Hydrodynamics [10]) is another mini-app. It is representative of 3D Lagrangian hydrodynamics on an unstructured mesh. It is a very popular application when used as a benchmark due to its characteristics and the opportunities that it brings in terms of generating load-imbalances in processors [9]. For our tests, we focused on the pure MPI version of the code. We had to use 64 tasks on a KNL node. We set the number of elements in the mesh to 24 (using the `-s` argument).

4.2   Workflow Implementation

Next, we ran the different steps in our workflow. This section details the results that we achieved for those applications.

4.2.1   Identify Memory Requirements

We first ran all the benchmarks on a KNL node configured in "Flat SNC-4" mode. This mode exposes the available memory (DDR4 and MCDRAM) as a total of 8 NUMA nodes: the first four nodes [0–3] are DDR4, while the last four [4–7] belong to MCDRAM. By default, the memory is allocated on DDR4 if no modification in the code or in the NUMA affinity is introduced. The results can be seen in Fig. 2. This figure shows the amount of memory allocated on each NUMA node throughout the execution time of each application. For example, for MiniMD it can be seen how approximately 2.5 GB are allocated on Node 0, 1.3 GB on Node 1, 1.7 GB on Node 2, 1.2 GB on Node 3, and no data is allocated on the other 4 NUMA nodes (MCDRAM). Since we are running applications with enough MPI tasks to have at least one task per NUMA node, all four DDR4 NUMA nodes are used. The MPI library sets the placement of the task and then the operating system allocates the memory on the closest NUMA node. Overall, the memory utilization remains constant until the end of the execution when it is deallocated. Similar behaviour can be observed for all the applications presented in the paper.

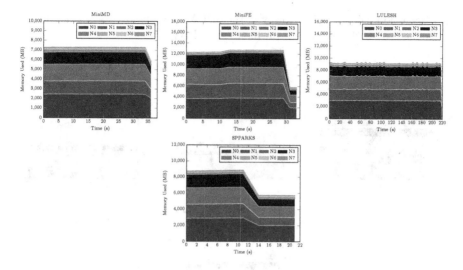

Fig. 2. NUMA utilization for all applications running in "Flat SNC4" mode with default settings

4.2.2 Analyze NUMA Utilization and Fix NUMA Bindings

In the previous experiment all the test cases ran using DDR4 only. We also observed that for all the test cases, the memory footprint was smaller than 16 GB, which makes these test cases as ideal candidates for running directly from MCDRAM. Next, we will show the results of running the test cases using MCDRAM only. For applications with multiple MPI tasks per node, it is necessary for users to introduce additional steps to fix the affinity of the processes involved in the computation so that the MCDRAM NUMA node that is closest to them is used. For these tests, we have used a KNL node configured in **Flat SNC4** mode, which exposes a total of 8 NUMA nodes.

Our workflow captures the CPU usage when each task is executed, and instructs **numactl** to set the appropriate memory policy for the task. Initially, all data is stored in the local MCDRAM node. Once it is full, the remaining data is allocated in the local DDR4 node. Indeed, this approach works optimally when all the data fits within the MCDRAM. However, it might put key data structures on the DDR4 if the memory footprint is large enough. Our workflow covers this scenario by analyzing the placement of individual data structures.

Figure 3 shows the memory utilization on each NUMA node throughout the execution time for each test case. It can be seen that after fixing the affinity on the basis of the recommendation of the tools in our workflow, the applications effectively use the available MCDRAM nodes rather than the DDR4 nodes. It is also worth noticing that the execution time has significantly decreased for all the test cases as a result of the increased memory bandwidth provided by the MCDRAM. All the test cases show a behavior similar to what was previously described when using DDR4. However, the SPPARKS memory footprint changed significantly with the change in problem/model type.

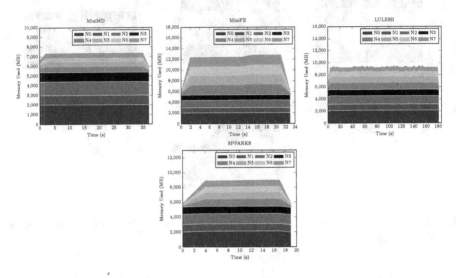

Fig. 3. NUMA utilization for all codes after fixing the affinity

Left plot in Fig. 4 shows the hits on the different NUMA nodes for LULESH after correctly setting the affinity on the basis of the recommendations of the tool. It can be seen how all hits are to MCDRAM NUMA nodes instead of DDR4 nodes. For comparison, the plot on the right shows the hits on the different MCDRAM nodes when only `numactl` is used globally for all tasks (naive approach, as in `mpirun numactl --membind=4,5,6,7 ./lulesh2.0`). In the second case, while all the NUMA hits still take place on MCDRAM nodes, they all hit the first MCDRAM node. Many of those hits are remote hits. This is equivalent to incurring NUMA misses. We can see how the execution time is higher in the figure on the right as a result of these misses.

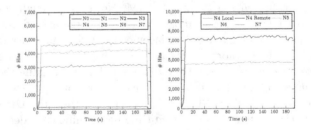

Fig. 4. NUMA utilization

4.3   Selecting Relevant MCDRAM Configurations

We ran the test cases on KNL nodes configured in different memory and cluster modes. In this section we present the results of running the test cases in (1) cache-quadrant mode (i.e., MCDRAM is configured for usage as an L3 cache, and the KNL tiles are logically divided in four parts which are spatially local to the four groups of memory controllers); (2) flat-quadrant mode (i.e., MCDRAM is configured for usage as addressable memory that complements DDR4, and the KNL tiles are logically divided in four parts which are spatially local to the four groups of memory controllers); and (3) flat-SNC4 mode (i.e., MCDRAM is configured for usage as addressable memory that complements DDR4, and the KNL tiles are divided into four separate NUMA nodes).

The tool that we use at this step (ICAT) follows an iterative process as depicted in Fig. 5. For the purpose of this paper, we focus on the options in the tool that are relevant for memory optimization. The user interacts with the tool after each step, agreeing on continuing or answering simple questions. At the end of the execution of the tool, a set of recommendations are presented. The users can implement these recommendations to improve the performance of the code. The recommendations include the best memory/cluster mode to be used as well as instructions for improving the memory bindings of the target code.

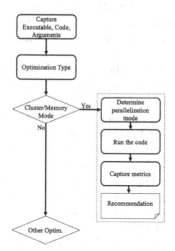

Fig. 5. Iterative process for generation of memory/cluster mode configuration

The results shown in Table 1 depict the best KNL configuration for running the different applications according to ICAT. This saves the user from spending time and effort in discovering those modes by trial-and-error, and without feeling burdened about the information on the low-level microarchitectural details of the processor and the application characteristics. Table 1 also shows how, for the case of SPPARKS (we include two different use cases, a large run and a short one), the results for the large run do not follow the recommendation. This is due to the nature of the problem being solved, with a set of random components that directly impact the overall execution time.

Table 1. Performance comparison of test cases run in different memory and cluster modes - Run-time in seconds used for comparison.

Application	Recommendation	Cache-Quad	Flat-Quad	Flat-SNC4
MiniMD	Flat/Cache-Quadrant	34.688	40.930	36.125
MiniFE	Flat-SNC4	64.768	45.743	44.538
LULESH	Flat/Cache-Quadrant	315.083	328.459	514.193
SPPARKS small	Flat/Cache-Quadrant	18.878	17.501	23.022
SPPARKS large	Flat/Cache-Quadrant	2314.830	2260.723	**1812.511**

4.4 Code Adaptation

Code re-engineering may be necessary for improving the parallelization and vectorization of applications ported to systems with deep-memory hierarchies. Memory optimization of the application may also be required. As previously described, on the basis of an application's characteristics, one of our tools in the workflow, ICAT, can advise the user on modifying, compiling, and optimally running the application on the KNL processors. If a user desires, our tool can also automatically modify the application code for implementing any required changes for using the `hbwmalloc` interface, and thereby can help in optimally using the MCDRAM.

As previously stated, the memory footprint for all our test cases was less than 16 GB, therefore, all the data fitted into the MCDRAM. In such scenarios, as previously shown, usually the applications can be run optimally by allocating the required data on the MCDRAM. However, since the MCDRAM latency is higher than that of DDR4, applications with latency-sensitive data structures and memory access patterns would see a penalty when all the data structures are allocated on MCDRAM. For such latency-sensitive applications, a combination of MCDRAM and DDR4, where the latency sensitive data structures are allocated into DDR4, would offer the best performance. Moreover, there can be several applications that may benefit by prioritizing the assignment of large data structures to the MCDRAM - that is, the data structure/s that will be used for a longer duration over the lifetime of a program and are $\leq$ 16 GB in size can be assigned higher priority for assignment in the MCDRAM. However, upon experimentation, we found that none of the applications selected as test cases for this paper fall into this category.

Nonetheless, for demonstrating the code re-engineering capabilities of the tool present in our workflow, we chose the *"openmp-opt-knl"* version of the MiniFE application despite knowing that our tool advised that no such re-engineering is required. Hence, we do not expect any significant improvement in the application performance by using the `hbwmalloc` interface.

The Mantevo benchmark suite already contains a version of the MiniFE code that is capable of allocating the memory of selected data structures on the MCDRAM using the `memkind` interface - the *"openmp-opt-knl-memkind"* version. We show that the performance of the code generated by our tool (that re-engineers the *"openmp-opt-knl"* version to use the `hbwmalloc` interface) is comparable to this version of the MiniFE code that uses the `memkind` interface. It should be noted that both the `memkind` interface and the `hbwmalloc` interface are supported by the same `memkind` library. The results of the comparison are presented in Table 2. Since the MiniFE application performed best on the KNL nodes configured in the Flat memory mode and SNC4 cluster mode, we used this mode for the results in Table 2. It is worth noticing that without requiring the users to introduce any changes in the code, our tool can help them in adapting their applications to optimally take advantage of the `hbwmalloc` interface without incurring any significant loss in performance.

Table 2. Run-time comparison of different versions of MiniFE.

Version	Time (s)
openmp-opt-knl	45.73
openmp-opt-knl-memkind	46.26
re-engineered-openmp-opt-knl	45.922

5 Conclusions

While hardware manufactures release innovative chip designs and memory hierarchies for powering science and discoveries, the users of those chips should not be burdened by the continuous need to manually update application code to take advantage of the innovative hardware features. Hence, high-productivity workflows and tools are needed. In this paper, we have presented one such high-productivity workflow that helps the users in efficiently utilizing the deep-memory hierarchies. Our workflow can be used on existing petascale supercomputers as demonstrated in this paper. The workflow, and eventually the tools that comprise the workflow, free the users from the burden of learning about low-level microarchitectural details of the deep-memory hierarchies during the process of porting their applications to supercomputers.

We have demonstrated the applicability of our approach to commonly used HPC applications as well as to the benchmarks that are representative of the workloads on the supercomputers at several open-science data centers. The results show that we are able to achieve performance comparable to applications optimized by experts.

We have adopted a user-centric approach for implementing our workflow. Instead of offering complex tools with significant overheads and convoluted metrics, we offer a workflow that is easy to implement and that can be applied to a large number of applications. The workflow is suitable for running HPC applications developed using the most common programming languages and models, and involves tools that are available for public usage. We plan to do the usability analysis of our tools and the workflow in future. We also plan on expanding the capabilities of the tools in our workflow to support additional hardware elements like non-volatile memories.

Acknowledgment. We are very grateful to the National Science Foundation for grant #1642396, ICERT REU program (National Science Foundation grant #1359304), XSEDE (National Science Foundation grant #ACI-1053575), and Texas Advanced Computing Center (TACC) for providing resources required for this project. We are grateful to Tiffany Connors and Lars Koesterke for their contributions to the ICAT codebase. Stampede2 is generously funded by the National Science Foundation (NSF) through award ACI-1540931.

References

1. Arora, R., Koesterke, L.: Interactive code adaptation tool for modernizing applications for Intel knights landing processors. In: Proceedings of the Practice and Experience in Advanced Research Computing 2017 on Sustainability, Success and Impact, PEARC 2017, pp. 28:1–28:8. ACM, New York (2017). DOI https://doi.org/10.1145/3093338.3093352
2. Chandrasekar, K., Ni, X., Kale, L.V.: A memory heterogeneity-aware runtime system for bandwidth-sensitive HPC applications. In: 2017 IEEE International Parallel and Distributed Processing Symposium Workshops (IPDPSW), pp. 1293–1300 (2017). https://doi.org/10.1109/IPDPSW.2017.168
3. Harrod, W.: A journey to exascale computing. In: 2012 SC Companion on High Performance Computing, Networking, Storage and Analysis (SCC), pp. 1702–1730. IEEE (2012)
4. Hartmann, C., Fey, D.: An extended analysis of memory hierarchies for efficient implementations of image processing applications. J. R.-Time Image Process. (2017). https://doi.org/10.1007/s11554-017-0723-2
5. Hennessy, J.L., Patterson, D.A.: Computer Architecture: A Quantitative Approach, 5th edn. Morgan Kaufmann Publishers Inc., San Francisco (2011)
6. Heroux, M.A., et al.: Improving performance via mini-applications. Technical report SAND2009-5574, Sandia National Laboratories, Albuquerque, New Mexico 87185 and Livermore, California 94550 (2009)
7. Intel: Memkind (2017). http://memkind.github.io/memkind/. Accessed 25 Jun 2018
8. Jun, H., et al.: HBM (High Bandwidth Memory) DRAM technology and architecture. In: 2017 IEEE International Memory Workshop (IMW), pp. 1–4 (2017). https://doi.org/10.1109/IMW.2017.7939084

9. Karlin, I., et al.: Exploring traditional and emerging parallel programming models using a proxy application. In: Proceedings of the 2013 IEEE 27th International Symposium on Parallel and Distributed Processing, IPDPS 2013, pp. 919–932. IEEE Computer Society, Washington, DC (2013). https://doi.org/10.1109/IPDPS.2013.115

10. Karlin, I., Keasler, J., Neely, J.: Lulesh 2.0 updates and changes. Technical report, Lawrence Livermore National Laboratory (LLNL), Livermore, CA (2013)

11. Khaldi, D., Chapman, B.: Towards automatic HBM allocation using LLVM: a case study with knights landing. In: Proceedings of the Third Workshop on LLVM Compiler Infrastructure in HPC, LLVM-HPC 2016, pp. 12–20. IEEE Press, Piscataway (2016). https://doi.org/10.1109/LLVM-HPC.2016.7

12. Laboratory, S.N.: Mantevo Project Homepage (2018). http://mantevo.org. Accessed 25 June 2018

13. Peng, I.B., Gioiosa, R., Kestor, G., Cicotti, P., Laure, E., Markidis, S.: RTHMS: a tool for data placement on hybrid memory system. In: Proceedings of the 2017 ACM SIGPLAN International Symposium on Memory Management, ISMM 2017, pp. 82–91. ACM, New York (2017). https://doi.org/10.1145/3092255.3092273

14. Plimpton, S., et al.: Crossing the mesoscale no-man's land via parallel kinetic Monte Carlo (2009)

15. PRACE: Partnership for Advanced Computing in Europe (2018). http://www.prace-ri.eu/. Accessed 25 June 2018

16. Reinders, J.: VTune Performance Analyzer Essentials. Intel Press (2005)

17. Rosales, C., et al.: A comparative study of application performance and scalability on the Intel knights landing processor. In: Taufer, M., Mohr, B., Kunkel, J.M. (eds.) ISC High Performance 2016. LNCS, vol. 9945, pp. 307–318. Springer, Cham (2016). https://doi.org/10.1007/978-3-319-46079-6_22

18. Rosales, C., Gómez-Iglesias, A., Predoehl, A.: REMORA: a resource monitoring tool for everyone. In: Proceedings of the Second International Workshop on HPC User Support Tools, HUST 2015, pp. 3:1–3:8. ACM, New York (2015). https://doi.org/10.1145/2834996.2834999

19. Rosales, C., et al.: KNL utilization guidelines. Technical report TR-16-03, Texas Advanced Computing Center, Austin, Texas (2013)

20. Sodani, A.: Knights Landing (KNL): 2nd generation Intel Xeon Phi processor. In: 2015 IEEE Hot Chips 27 Symposium (HCS), pp. 1–24 (2015). https://doi.org/10.1109/HOTCHIPS.2015.7477467

21. Stanzione, D., et al.: Stampede 2: the evolution of an XSEDE supercomputer. In: Proceedings of the Practice and Experience in Advanced Research Computing 2017 on Sustainability, Success and Impact, PEARC 2017, pp. 15:1–15:8. ACM, New York (2017). https://doi.org/10.1145/3093338.3093385

22. Towns, J., et al.: XSEDE: accelerating scientific discovery. Comput. Sci. Eng. **16**(5), 62–74 (2014). https://doi.org/10.1109/MCSE.2014.80

Semi-automatic Code Modernization
for Optimal Parallel I/O

Ritu Arora[1(✉)] and Trung Nguyen Ba[2]

[1] Texas Advanced Computing Center, University of Texas at Austin,
Austin, TX, USA
rauta@tacc.utexas.edu
[2] University of Massachusetts at Amherst, Amherst, MA, USA
tnguyenba@cs.umass.edu

Abstract. As we progress from the multi-petascale era to the exascale computing era, the need for optimally doing parallel I/O will become increasingly important not only for enhancing the performance of an application, but also for the health of the underlying systems on which the applications run. Manual reengineering of existing applications to optimally do I/O can be challenging for several parallel programmers despite the availability of the MPI I/O interface, high-level APIs and libraries (such as parallel HDF5, and parallel NetCDF). In this paper, we present an interactive, high-level tool for reengineering existing applications so that they can do parallel I/O optimally. This tool frees the developers from the effort required for manually reengineering their applications to take advantage of the MPI libraries and the Lustre filesystem, and hence, helps in enhancing their productivity. Parallelizing I/O using our tool does not involve any external high-level I/O library, is purely MPI based, helps in optimally using the Lustre filesystem when it is available, and results in code that is portable across different systems supporting MPI libraries. The performance of the code generated using our tool is comparable to the performance of the best available manually written versions of the code for the selected test cases.

1 Introduction

Scientific applications typically read or write data. For example, they could be reading initial datasets for processing, writing numerical data from simulations, and writing application-level checkpoints. The reading or writing of data from the applications is called I/O. For maximizing an application's performance, one should not only consider optimizing the computation and communication time consumed by the application but also the time spent in doing the I/O. As we progress from the multi-petascale to exascale computing era, the scale of I/O from the applications running at large-scale is also likely to increase, and hence, it will become critical to do optimal I/O. However, doing efficient I/O without stressing out the underlying filesystems can be challenging and is often an afterthought.

© Springer Nature Singapore Pte Ltd. 2019
A. Majumdar and R. Arora (Eds.): SCEC 2018, CCIS 964, pp. 140–154, 2019.
https://doi.org/10.1007/978-981-13-7729-7_10

At open-science supercomputing facilities, the parallel distributed filesystems are shared resources, and typically, there are several hundred users who could be accessing a filesystem simultaneously for reading and writing data from their applications or scripts. If users open and close files too frequently when running applications at a large-scale, or create too many small files too often, they can stress out the metadata server that helps in negotiating the connection of applications with the server controlling the physical storage media on which the files should be written or read from. Hence, due to such activity of even one user, the entire filesystem can become unavailable to all the users on the system and all the jobs running on the system will start failing. Therefore, doing efficient I/O is not only critical for performance reasons but is also important for maintaining good citizenship on a supercomputer.

I/O efficiency and hence the I/O performance can be controlled at the parallel filesystem level by setting some properties like file stripe count and file stripe size, and also by doing file reads and writes in parallel from within the applications. On the parallel distributed filesystems built using Lustre [14], the users are allowed to change the settings of a file's stripe size and stripe count [6] at the time of the file-creation. Each file stripe is a block of a fixed size and the stripe count coveys the number of storage targets (or disks) on which the stripes should be accomodated. Lustre allows striping a file across 2000 storage targets (or disks), and each storage object (or a piece of the file) can be up to 16 TBs in size. By striping a file across multiple storage targets, one can create multiple I/O channels for accessing the file. As each access channel is controlled by a different server, the available I/O bandwidth will increase and lead to the performance improvement for file I/O. Also, by placing chunks of a file on multiple storage targets, the space required by the file is not restricted by the size of a single storage target (or disk). Even though it is easy to implement file striping and setting stripe size either through command-line or by invoking some functions from within an application at the time of creating the file, these features seem to be usually overlooked by HPC software developers and users.

The Message Passing Interface (MPI) I/O functions provide a scalable and portable approach for doing efficient parallel I/O. It provides over 50 function calls/routines for supporting parallel I/O and includes the capabilities such as collective I/O, nonblocking collective I/O, and noncontiguous I/O [5]. It also provides a mechanism for providing hints for setting the file stripe size and file stripe count for the Lustre filesystem. While the MPI I/O interface has advantages related to performance, portability, and scalability, using it may not be straightforward in already existing applications as manual reengineering of existing applications to replace the serial I/O with parallel I/O may be required. This can be an effort-intensive activity for many programmers.

In the light of the aforementioned discussion, the questions that arise are: (1) can we have a high-level approach for using MPI I/O such that we can ensure programmer productivity, application portability, and code maintainability? (2) at the time of file creation, can we pass hints to the Lustre file system for setting a file's stripe size and stripe count using a high-level interface? To address these questions, and to help those interested in learning about MPI I/O, we have extended the Interactive Parallelization Tool (IPT) [2] to add support for MPI

I/O and Lustre file stripe count/size adjustment. Thus, with the help of the latest features supported in IPT, the users can not only convert serial I/O to parallel I/O using the MPI I/O interface but can also adjust some settings on the Lustre filesystem.

In the rest of this paper, we present an overview of the work done to add the parallel I/O support in IPT. We demonstrate the process of using IPT for parallel I/O. We also include the data related to the evaluation of this new feature and present future work that will be undertaken on this topic.

2 High-Level Overview of IPT and Its Support for Parallel I/O

IPT is an interactive tool that helps the users in semi-automatically transforming serial programs into parallel programs and supports the MPI, OpenMP, and CUDA programming models. IPT parses the input programs, prompts the users for the necessary information regarding the parallelization of their serial programs, and does source-to-source transformation for generating a parallel version of the applications. Figure 1 shows a pictorial high-level overview of the different components in IPT.

As shown in Fig. 1, IPT uses the ROSE compiler [11] as its code transformation engine. It has in-built rules and design templates that capture the knowledge of expert parallel programmers. These rules and design templates are written in C++ for each of the following programming models: MPI, OpenMP, and CUDA. The relevant rules and templates are invoked during the parallelization process on the basis of the specifications provided by the user. The input source code provided by the users remain unchanged, and IPT writes the parallel version in a new file. For converting serial I/O to parallel I/O using MPI and passing hints to the Lustre filesystem for appropriate file striping, the users should provide the specifications to IPT through an interactive question and answer system.

3 Code Transformation for Parallel I/O

IPT is capable of parallelizing I/O implementations in both serial and already parallel programs. The process of parallelizing I/O in serial and MPI programs using IPT involves the following steps:

1. **Soliciting specifications for parallel I/O:** The user interactively specifies the location of the I/O code that should be parallelized and on the basis of the user-specifications, IPT applies the appropriate in-built rules/heuristics for analyzing the I/O code.
2. **Checking constraints and analyses:** The specified I/O code is analyzed for dependencies. Each statement is checked and analyzed statically for certain patterns recognized by IPT. The statements are also checked for complex data structures that are not currently supported by IPT. Once all the constraints are specified, IPT prompts the user for further information regarding parallelizing the I/O.

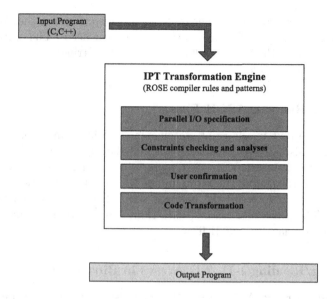

Fig. 1. IPT: high-level overview and structure.

3. **Confirmation from user:** IPT prompts the user to confirm the parallelization of the selected code blocks, and solicits further information about the
   type of parallel I/O that is required (selection of one type produces an ASCII
   file, and the other one produces a binary file), and the type of the filesystem
   on which the parallel code will do I/O.
4. **Code transformation:** After receiving user's confirmation, IPT reengineers
   the existing I/O code to insert the relevant code for using the MPI I/O interface, such as, the MPI header file, MPI function calls for I/O, statements for
   declaring variables and controlling the flow of the program, and modifying the
   existing statements. It generate a version of the code that supports MPI I/O.

There are certain constraints that the programs should meet so that they can be
parallelized using IPT. The first requirement is that there should be at least one
for-loop in which I/O is done serially. The presence of such a loop indicates that
there is enough work to engage more than one MPI process to do I/O. Another
requirement, which is due to a limitation in the current version of IPT, is that
these loops should not contain break statements, return statements, or nested
while-loops because these can break the logic of I/O load distribution among
the MPI processes engaged in doing I/O.

4 Types of I/O Patterns Supported by IPT

IPT can be used for inserting code for reading and writing both ASCII and
binary files from parallel applications. ASCII file format is typically chosen for
writing log data, and the binary file format is typically used for writing results

that can be post-processed by other tools. IPT users can select the appropriate option for writing files - ASCII or binary - as per their needs. The data in arrays can be written in both ASCII and binary formats. Strings can be written in ASCII format only though.

4.1   Writing/Reading ASCII Files

IPT converts the text in the print statements to strings, and stores them in a string buffer. It also adds code to keep track of the total length of the buffer in each MPI process. It inserts the code to determine the file offset for each process based on the total length of the string buffer. Finally, IPT inserts the MPI I/O calls in the program to write the buffered string from each MPI process to a common file. The process of reading data from ASCII files is the inverse of the process of writing data to ASCII files.

4.2   Writing/Reading 1-D, 2-D Arrays in Binary Files

Besides reading/writing ASCII data, IPT can also be used for optimally reading/writing 1-D and 2-D arrays in the binary format. Such reads and writes can be done without additional storage and computations. However, there are some constraints that should be satisfied. First, the I/O code block marked for parallelization needs to be a for-loop or a nested for-loop. Second, it needs to contain only serial I/O statements. In addition, the I/O statement should be reading/writing one element of the array at a time along with a separator. The examples of patterns that can be recognized by IPT are shown in Table 1. Note that the output file written by MPI I/O calls are in the binary format and can be read using appropriate MPI calls in the application. The data written is in the external32 format and is portable across different HPC platforms. In order to view the data written in these binary files from the command-line, the utilities like hexdump [8] can be used.

Table 1. Examples of I/O from 1-D and 2-D arrays that can be optimized.

Optimizable 1-D array I/O	Optimizable 2-D array I/O
```int a[100]; for (int i =0; i < 100;i++) { fprintf(f,"%d,",a[i]); }```	```int a[100][100]; for (int i =0; i < 100;i++) { for (int j =0; j < 100;j++) { fprintf(f,"%d,",a[i][j]); } }```

4.3   Setting File Stripe Size and Count for the Lustre Filesystem

IPT can help the users in setting appropriate stripe size and stripe count on the output files written from their applications so that these files can be stored across multiple storage targets across the Lustre filesystem. By striping the files appropriately, users can increases the I/O bandwidth available to them for accessing the files from parallel applications (at a later point) as there will be multiple channels to access the file. Striping the files across multiple storage targets will also help in avoiding data overflow on a single storage target (disk) in the case the output files are large.

5   Demonstrating the MPI I/O Support in IPT

In this section, we demonstrate the process of parallelizing I/O in serial and parallel programs. We have chosen very simple examples for this demonstration, and the code of these examples is shown in Table 2. We will present a walk-through of the process of using IPT to parallelize the code in these tables.

Table 2. Input program code snippets.

Serial 1-D writing	Serial 1-D reading
```int main () { FILE *f = NULL; int a[100]; for (int i =0; i < 100; i++) { a[i] = i; } f = fopen("test.txt","w+"); for (int i =0; i < 100;i++) { fprintf(f,"%d,",a[i]); } fclose(f); return 0; }```	```int main () { FILE *f; int a[100]; f = fopen("test.txt","r"); for (int i =0; i < 100; i++) { fscanf(f,"%d,",&a[i]); } fclose(f); return 0; }```

The IPT executable is invoked from command-line, and accepts the path to the input source code as an argument. As soon as IPT starts running, it prompts the user to select one of the three parallel programming models that it supports: MPI, OpenMP and CUDA. Table 3, shows this prompt and also shows that we have selected the MPI programming model as we are interested in inserting the code for MPI I/O in the input source code.

Table 3. Step 1: selecting a parallel programming model.

```
Please select a parallel programming model from the following available options:
1. MPI
2. OpenMP
3. CUDA
1
```

As a next step, the users are prompted to specify whether the input code is an already existing MPI program or not. Since we started with a serial program, we choose "no" for this question prompt and this is shown in Table 4.

Table 4. Step 2: selecting program type.

Is this an MPI program (y/n)?
n

The IPT users can either parallelize just the I/O in their existing applications or can parallelize both computation and I/O. Depending upon their preference for one of these options to parallelize I/O in their applications, the users can select the appropriate patterns for parallelizing I/O and computations. The MPI programming related patterns that are currently supported by IPT are shown in Table 5. Depending upon the chosen option, different control statements are inserted in the generated code. In this example, since we only want to demonstrate the MPI I/O support in IPT, we select the independent pattern that supports MPI I/O (option 10).

Table 5. Step 3: selecting the pattern for parallelization.

Please select a pattern from the following list that best characterizes your parallelization needs:
(Please refer to the user-guide for the explanation on each of the patterns, and note that not all the listed patterns may be relevant for your application type.)
1. For-Loop Parallelization
2. Stencil
3. Pipeline
4. Data Distribution and Data Collection
5. Data Distribution
6. Data Collection
7. Point to Point
8. Master-worker pattern - Data distribution - Broadcast
9. MPI environment initialization and finalization
10. MPI parallel I/O
10

IPT supports file striping for the Lustre filesystem. In the next step, IPT prompts the users if they are interested in writing data in parallel, and if they require support for striping the output file on a Lustre filesystem. If the users select the option of file striping, IPT prompts for additional information related to the stripe count and size. IPT does not handle errors related to the incorrect specifications provided by the users (e.g., if the output file chosen for striping already exists). For parallelizing the process of writing a 1-D array (code-sample shown in Table 2), we choose "yes" for the option of doing file striping on the Lustre filesystem (Table 6).

Table 6. Step 4: selecting the file striping option for running code on the Lustre filesystem.

Do you want to do file striping on the Lustre filesystem (Y/N)??
Y
Please enter the stripe count (the number of storage targets across which you would like to spread the file storage):
4
Please enter number of stripe size (in MB):
4

The next step is to choose the blocks of I/O code that should be parallelized. IPT generates a file that contains the intermediate version of the input code with line-numbers. It then prompts the user to provide the line-numbers that contain the serial I/O code which should be parallelized. In order for IPT to work correctly, the chosen blocks of code need to include all the statements related to the output file (e.g., statements for file open, file close, and file I/O). Even though IPT is implemented to handle the cases where some of these statements are not provided in the user-specification, it is a good practice to include all of them. For the sample intermediate code shown in Table 7, the user will need to choose all statements from line #10 to line #14. After the blocks of I/O code are selected, IPT will automatically detect the statements that can be parallelized using MPI I/O.

Table 7. Step 5: selecting the blocks of code for parallelizing I/O.

Selecting the code region for writing to a file in parallel - MPI write	Selecting the code region for reading a file in parallel - MPI read
NOTE: To make sure that the process of writing and reading the data is successful, please indicate the lines of code that is used to perform file I/O in the original code.	NOTE: To make sure that the process of writing and reading the data is successful, please indicate the lines of code that is used to perform file I/O in the original code.
For your convenience we have generated a file called numberedCode.C with line numbers corresponding to each line of your code. You can chose to show this file here or open this file in a different terminal. Do you want to show the file ? (Y/N) **Y**	For your convenience we have generated a file called numberedCode.C with line numbers corresponding to each line of your code. You can chose to show this file here or open this file in a different terminal. Do you want to show the file ? (Y/N) **Y**

0 : int rose_size;
1 : int rose_rank;
2 : FILE *f =((void *)0);
3 : int a[100];
4 : MPI_Init(NULL,NULL);
5 : MPI_Comm_size(MPI_COMM_WORLD , & rose_size);
6 : MPI_Comm_rank(MPI_COMM_WORLD , & rose_rank);
7 : for (int i = 0;;;i < 100;;i++) {
8 : a[i] = i;
9 : }
10 : f = fopen("test.txt","w+");
11 : for (int i = 0;;;i < 100;;i++) {
12 : fprintf(f,"%d,",a[i]);
13 : }
14 : fclose(f);
15 : MPI_Finalize();
16 : return 0;
 	
Select the line numbers from the Number-Code.txt file in which you want to perform the operation, and enter the line numbers here (format:[a],[a-b],[a,b]).
10-14
	0 : int rose_size;
	1 : int rose_rank;
	2 : FILE *f;
	3 : int a[100];
	4 : MPI_Init(NULL,NULL);
	5 : MPI_Comm_size(MPI_COMM_WORLD , & rose_size);
	6 : MPI_Comm_rank(MPI_COMM_WORLD , & rose_ rank);
	7 : f = fopen("test.txt","r");
	8 : for (int i = 0;;;i < 100;;i++) {
	9 : fscanf(f,"%d,",&a[i]);
	10 : }
	11 : fclose(f);
	12 : MPI_Finalize();
	13 : return 0;
	
	Select the line numbers from the Number-Code.txt file in which you want to perform the operation, and enter the line numbers here (format:[a],[a-b],[a,b]).
	7-11

Similarly, when parallelizing the code for reading a file, users need to choose the blocks of I/O code that they want to parallelize. They should include all the statements related to the input files in these blocks. For the example presented in this paper, statements from line #7 to line #11 as shown in Table 7 are chosen. After the I/O blocks are selected, IPT will automatically parallelize all the appropriate statements in those blocks.

Since IPT supports both ASCII and binary I/O, the users should select one of them depending upon their applications' needs. For writing 1-D arrays or 2-D arrays to a file, users are prompted to choose the type of output (ASCII or binary). Different statements are inserted into the input source code depending upon the ASCII or binary file types as selected by the users. In the example presented in this paper, we select the option of writing a binary file - please see Table 8.

Table 8. Step 6: selecting MPI I/O type.

Selecting type of MPI write	Selecting type of MPI read

Selecting MPI I/O type for writing to a file
The loop:
 	
for (int i = 0; i < 100; i++) {
fprintf(f,"%d,",a[i]);
}
is identified to be a candidate for MPI I/O with ASCII output. Do you want to perform this operation ? (y/n)
y
The loop:
 	
for (int i = 0; i < 100; i++) {
fprintf(f,"%d,",a[i]);
}
is identified to be a candidate for MPI I/O with binary output. Do you want to perform this operation ? (y/n)
y
Doing MPI collective I/O with binary output
	The loop:
	
	for (int i = 0; i < 100; i++) {
	fscanf(f,"%d,",&a[i]);
	}
	is identified to be a candidate for MPI I/O with binary input. Do you want to perform this operation ? (y/n)
	y

Similar to the process of writing files using MPI I/O, while reading files using MPI I/O, the users need to specify the file type - ASCII or binary. In the example presented in this paper, we selected the option of reading a binary file - see Table 8.

The generated parallel programs that are capable of doing parallel I/O are shown in Table 9. As can be noticed from this table, IPT first converted the serial programs into MPI programs, and then updated the code for serial I/O to use MPI I/O. The contents of the binary file produced by the parallelized code are shown in Table 10. These contents were displayed using `hexdump` and they are similar to that written by the serial program. Also, as shown in Table 11, the MPI version of the program for reading data from an existing file works correctly and this can be checked by comparing the data that it reads with the data read by the serial version of the program.

6   Evaluation

We tested the code generated for the test cases presented in this paper on the Stampede2 supercomputer [17]. Stampede2 is equipped with both Intel Knights

Table 9. Code generated by IPT for parallel I/O.

Parallel MPI writing	Parallel MPI reading
| ```c
#include <stdio.h>
#include "stdlib.h"
#include <mpi.h>
int main()
{
  int rose_size;
  int rose_rank;
  FILE *f = ((void *)0);
  int a[100];
  MPI_Init(NULL,NULL);
  MPI_Comm_size(MPI_COMM_WORLD,&rose_size);
  for (int i = 0; i < 100; i++) {
    a[i] = i;
  }
if(rose_rank==0) {
system("lfs setstripe -c 4 test.txt");
  f = fopen("test.txt","w+");
}
{
if (rose_rank == 0) { fclose(f);}
MPI_Info a_info;
MPI_Info_create(&a_info);
MPI_Info_set(a_info,"stripping_factor","4");
MPI_File a_MPI;
MPI_File_open(MPI_COMM_WORLD,"test.txt",
      MPI_MODE_CREATE|MPI_MODE_WRONLY|MPI_MODE_APPEND
      ,a_info, &a_MPI);
MPI_Offset a_initial_offset;
MPI_File_get_position(a_MPI,&a_initial_offset);
int a_displacement [rose_size];
int a_recvcounts [rose_size];
int a_range = (100 - 0)/rose_size;
for (int rose_index = 0; rose_index < rose_size;
    rose_index++) {
 a_displacement [rose_index] = a_initial_offset +
     rose_index * (a_range);
 a_recvcounts [rose_index] = (rose_index == rose_size
     - 1) ? 100 +   a_initial_offset -
     a_displacement [rose_index] : a_range;
}
MPI_File_write_at_all(a_MPI,a_displacement[rose_rank
   ]*sizeof(MPI_INT),a + rose_rank * a_range,
    a_recvcounts[rose_rank],MPI_INT,
    MPI_STATUS_IGNORE);
 MPI_Info_free(&a_info);
MPI_File_close(&a_MPI);
if (rose_rank == 0) { f = fopen("test.txt","a");}
}
if(rose_rank==0) {
  fclose(f);
}
 MPI_Finalize();
 return 0;
}
``` | ```c
#include <stdio.h>
#include "stdlib.h"
#include <mpi.h>
int main()
{
  int rose_size;
  int rose_rank;
  FILE *f;
  int a[100];
  MPI_Init(NULL,NULL);
  MPI_Comm_size(MPI_COMM_WORLD,&rose_size);
  MPI_Comm_rank(MPI_COMM_WORLD,&rose_rank);
if(rose_rank==0) {
system("lfs setstripe -c 4 test.txt");
  f = fopen("test.txt","r");
}
{
int a_initial_offset = 0;
if (rose_rank == 0) { a_initial_offset = ftell(f);
    fclose(f);}
MPI_Request a_request;
MPI_Ibcast(&a_initial_offset,1, MPI_INT, 0,
      MPI_COMM_WORLD,&a_request);
MPI_File a_MPI;
MPI_File_open(MPI_COMM_WORLD,"test.txt",
      MPI_MODE_RDONLY,MPI_INFO_NULL, &a_MPI);
MPI_File_seek(a_MPI,a_initial_offset,MPI_SEEK_SET);
MPI_File_read_at_all(a_MPI,a_initial_offset,a,100,
      MPI_INT,MPI_STATUS_IGNORE);
MPI_Offset  a_current_offset;
MPI_File_get_position(a_MPI,&a_current_offset);
int a_read_offset =  a_current_offset;
MPI_File_close(&a_MPI);
if (rose_rank == 0) {
f = fopen("test.txt","r");
fseek(f,a_read_offset,SEEK_SET);
}
}
if(rose_rank==0) {
  fclose(f);
}
  MPI_Finalize();
  return 0;
}
``` |

Table 10. Writing data in parallel from the program generated by IPT versus reading the data in the serial program.

Output file written from the MPI program (read using hexdump)	Output file written by the serial version of the program
0 1 2 3 4 5 6 7 8 9 10 11 12 13 14 15 16 17 18 19 20 21 22 23 24 25 26 27 28 29 30 31 32 33 34 35 36 37 38 39 40 41 42 43 44 45 46 47 48 49 50 51 52 53 54 55 56 57 58 59 60 61 62 63 64 65 66 67 68 69 70 71 72 73 74 75 76 77 78 79 80 81 82 83 84 85 86 87 88 89 90 91 92 93 94 95 96 97 98 99	0,1,2,3,4,5,6,7,8,9,10,11,12,13,14,15,16,17,18,19, 20,21,22,23,24,25,26,27,28,29,30,31,32,33,34,35, 36,37,38,39,40,41,42,43,44,45,46,47,48,49,50,51, 52,53,54,55,56,57,58,59,60,61,62,63,64,65,66,67, 68,69,70,71,72,73,74,75,76,77,78,79,80,81,82,83, 84,85,86,87,88,89,90,91,92,93,94,95,96,97,98,99

Table 11. Reading data in parallel from the program generated by IPT versus reading the data in the serial program.

Array read from a file using the parallel MPI I/O	Array read from a file using the serial program
a[0] is 0 a[1] is 1 a[2] is 2 ... a[47] is 47 a[48] is 48 a[49] is 49 ... a[97] is 97 a[98] is 98 a[99] is 99	a[0] is 0 a[1] is 1 a[2] is 2 ... a[47] is 47 a[48] is 48 a[49] is 49 ... a[97] is 97 a[98] is 98 a[99] is 99

Landing (KNL) nodes and the Skylake nodes. We ran our tests on the KNL nodes. These nodes are equipped with high-bandwidth memory that can act as an L3 cache. The operating system can transparently use the L3 cache to move data from the main memory. In addition to this L3 cache, 96GB of RAM (on DDR4) was also available to the applications.

Let us consider four serial programs in which we parallelize I/O using IPT. Each of these programs are written in the C programming language and involve reading and writing data from files. We compared the parallel (MPI) versions of these programs that were generated by IPT with the versions that were hand-written for doing parallel I/O. The four example programs entailed: (1) file I/O for reading the values of 1-D integer array with 100,000,000 elements, (2) file I/O for writing the values of 1-D integer array with 100,000,000 elements, (3) file I/O for reading 2-D integer array with 10,000 × 10,000 elements, and (4) file I/O for writing a 2-D integer array with 10,000 × 10,000 elements.

As can be noticed from the data presented in Table 12, the performance of the hand-written parallel versions of the examples considered here is similar to the versions that were generated using IPT. The small variation in the execution time of the generated and the hand-written versions can be attributed to the fact that IPT inserts extra lines of the code to maintain the overall correctness of the generated program (in a general way). These statements are for handling load-imbalance between MPI processes, handling serial file I/O calls (ones that are not included in the parallelized code), and finding offset of the output file in case the output is appended an existing file. Due to these statements, the generated versions incur slightly extra run-time as compared to the manual version of the tests. However, as the problem size increases, the performance difference between the two parallel versions - generated and hand-written - decreases.

The number of lines of code inserted and modified by IPT to parallelize the I/O in the four examples is shown in Table 13, and is compared with the lines of code in the hand-written and serial versions of the examples. By comparing these lines of code, we can say that IPT reduced the manual effort involved in

Table 12. Run-time comparison of the different versions of the example programs.

Examples	Serial Time taken in seconds	IPT parallel Time taken in seconds *4 MPI processes used*	Manual parallel Time taken in seconds *4 MPI processes used*
1-D Array - reading	42	0.55	0.39
1-D Array - writing	54	1.7	1.66
2-D Array - reading	36	0.53	0.55
2-D Array - writing	40	1.71	1.74

Table 13. Comparison of the number of lines of code written manually and by IPT.

Examples	Serial Total #LoC	IPT parallel (#LoC Inserted-or-Deleted)/(#LoC)	Manual parallel (#LoC Inserted-or-Deleted)/(Total #LoC)
1-D Array - reading	11	Lines deleted: 3 Lines added: 32 Total number of lines: 40 %age of code change: 87.5	Lines deleted: 5 Lines added: 16 Total number of lines: 22 %age of code change: 95.5
1-D Array - writing	13	Lines deleted: 3 Lines added: 36 Total number of lines: 46 %age of code change: 84.7	Lines deleted: 6 Lines added: 15 Total number of lines: 22 %age of code change: 95.5
2-D Array - reading	13	Lines deleted: 5 Lines added: 30 Total number of lines: 38 %age of code change: 92.1	Lines deleted: 6 Lines added: 20 Total number of lines: 27 %age of code change: 96.3
2-D Array - writing	18	Lines deleted: 5 Lines added: 38 Total number of lines: 51 %age of code change: 84.3	Lines deleted: 7 Lines added: 24 Total number of lines: 35 %age of code change: 85.6

LoC = Lines of Code

parallelizing I/O in the programs by more than 80% on an average. Since IPT solicits the requirements for parallelizing I/O interactively and in plain/colloquial English, there is no significant learning curve involved in adopting IPT for generating parallel I/O code.

7   Related Work

Even though high-level libraries like parallel HDF5 [18] and NetCDF [13] are available for doing parallel I/O and they can also help in saving the file metadata within the files themselves, there is a learning curve associated with them and using them creates dependencies on external libraries, and thereby, can make the programmers worry about the portability and maintainability of the applications. In this section we discuss MPI based parallel I/O projects that are related to the work presented in this paper.

Significant efforts have been made to analyze the performance and scalability of the MPI applications doing parallel I/O. One example of such efforts is the work done by Latham *et al.* on the impact of MPI I/O on application scalability [12]. Focusing on other aspects, Shan and Shalf have created IOR, a benchmark to examine and analyze the performance of parallel I/O implementations [15]. Amongst the work done in recent years, Harrington *et al.* have demonstrated a method to capture bottleneck in parallel I/O calls [10]. These efforts and analyses show that developing applications with correct, efficient, and scalable parallel I/O is not a trivial task. Hence, there has always been a need for tools and techniques to help developer in taking advantages of parallel I/O.

Given the challenges in implementing correct, scalable, and efficient parallel I/O, multiple research projects have been undertaken as attempts to solve this issue. Corbett *et al.* have worked on comprehensive documentations, explanations, and examples for MPI I/O interfaces [7]. Bennett *et al.* have built Jovian, one of the earliest framework for optimizing parallel I/O for multi-cores machine architectures [3]. Focusing on implementing parallel I/O for checkpointing HPC programs, in their recent work, Arora *et al.* have proposed ITALC, an application level, non-invasive tool for checkpointing OpenMP and MPI programs [1]. Retrospect, an interactive debugger for parallel programs has been developed by Bouteiller *et al.* using parallel I/O as an unobstructive log-based mechanism [4]. These frameworks either require users to have significant knowledge about parallel I/O or are domain-specific. To the best of our knowledge, there are no openly accessible tools or frameworks for automatically or semi-automatically parallelizing the I/O in MPI applications.

8   Conclusions

Parallel I/O plays an important role in optimizing the performance of parallel programs. Even though high-level libraries that provide abstraction over MPI I/O exist (viz., ADIOS [9], PnetCDF [16], and HDF5), using these libraries also involves a learning curve and creates additional dependencies on third-party software. Therefore, we have extended IPT to support parallel I/O in existing serial and parallel applications. Using IPT, the HPC software developers can modernize their code to do parallel I/O, and learn about MPI I/O. Through the test cases presented in this paper, we have demonstrated that there is no significant difference in the performance of the parallel I/O code generated using IPT and the hand-written versions of the code. Moreover, the effort involved in using IPT to parallelize I/O is significantly low as compared to the effort involved in the manual parallelization of I/O. Tools like IPT can not only be useful in code modernization efforts but can also be used in education and training activities on parallel I/O.

Acknowledgement. The work presented in this paper was made possible through the National Science Foundation (NSF) award number 1642396. We are very grateful to NSF for the same.

References

1. Arora, R., Ba, T.N.: ITALC: interactive tool for application-level checkpointing. In: Proceedings of the Fourth International Workshop on HPC User Support Tools, HUST 2017, pp. 2:1–2:11. ACM, New York (2017). https://doi.org/10.1145/3152493.3152558

2. Arora, R., Olaya, J., Gupta, M.: A tool for interactive parallelization. In: Proceedings of the 2014 Annual Conference on Extreme Science and Engineering Discovery Environment, XSEDE 2014, pp. 51:1–51:8. ACM, New York (2014). https://doi.org/10.1145/2616498.2616558

3. Bennett, R., Bryant, K., Sussman, A., Das, R., Saltz, J.: Jovian: a framework for optimizing parallel I/O. In: Proceedings Scalable Parallel Libraries Conference, pp. 10–20, October 1994. https://doi.org/10.1109/SPLC.1994.377009

4. Bouteiller, A., Bosilca, G., Dongarra, J.: Retrospect: deterministic replay of MPI applications for interactive distributed debugging. In: Cappello, F., Herault, T., Dongarra, J. (eds.) EuroPVM/MPI 2007. LNCS, vol. 4757, pp. 297–306. Springer, Heidelberg (2007). https://doi.org/10.1007/978-3-540-75416-9_41. http://dl.acm.org/citation.cfm?id=2396095.2396148

5. Cazes, J., Arora, R.: Introduction to parallel I/O. https://www.tacc.utexas.edu/documents/13601/900558/MPI-IO-Final.pdf/eea9d7d3-4b81-471c-b244-41498070e35d. Accessed 20 Oct 2018

6. The University of Tennessee Knoxville: The National Institute for Computer Science: Lustre striping guide. https://www.nics.tennessee.edu/computing-resources/file-systems/lustre-striping-guide. Accessed 20 Oct 2018

7. Corbett, P., et al.: Overview of the MPI-IO parallel I/O interface (1995)

8. FreeBSD: HEXDUMP(1) FreeBSD General Commands Manual HEXDUMP(1). https://www.freebsd.org/cgi/man.cgi?query=hexdump&sektion=1. Accessed 20 Oct 2018

9. Gu, J., Klasky, S., Podhorszki, N., Qiang, J., Wu, K.: Querying large scientific data sets with adaptable IO system ADIOS. In: Yokota, R., Wu, W. (eds.) SCFA 2018. LNCS, vol. 10776, pp. 51–69. Springer, Cham (2018). https://doi.org/10.1007/978-3-319-69953-0_4

10. Harrington, P.: Diagnosing parallel I/O bottlenecks in HPC applications. In: International Conference for High Performance Computing Networking Storage and Analysis (SCI7) ACM Student Research Competition (SRC) (2017)

11. Quinlan, D.: Rose: compiler support for object-oriented frameworks. Parallel Process. Lett. **10**, 215–226 (2000)

12. Latham, R., Ross, R., Thakur, R.: The impact of file systems on MPI-IO scalability. In: Kranzlmüller, D., Kacsuk, P., Dongarra, J. (eds.) EuroPVM/MPI 2004. LNCS, vol. 3241, pp. 87–96. Springer, Heidelberg (2004). https://doi.org/10.1007/978-3-540-30218-6_18

13. NetCDF-UCAR: Network Common Data Form (NetCDF). https://www.hdfgroup.org/solutions/hdf5/. Accessed 20 Oct 2018

14. OpenSFS's Lustre: Luster. http://lustre.org/. Accessed 20 Oct 2018

15. Shan, H., Shalf, J.: Using IOR to analyze the I/O performance for HPC platforms. In: Cray User Group Conference, CUG 2007 (2007)

16. Texas Advanced Computing Center: PnetCDF: A Parallel I/O Library for NetCDF File Access. https://trac.mcs.anl.gov/projects/parallel-netcdf. Accessed 3 Dec 2018

17. Texas Advanced Computing Center: Stampede2 TACC'S Flagship Supercomputer. https://www.tacc.utexas.edu/systems/stampede2. Accessed 20 Oct 2018
18. The HDF5 Library & File Format: TheHDFGroup. https://www.hdfgroup.org/solutions/hdf5/. Accessed 20 Oct 2018

Author Index

Printed in the United States
By Bookmasters